D0915394

THE MOORHOUSE I. X. MILLAR LECTURE SERIES

PROSPERITY WITHOUT INFLATION • NUMBER ONE •
1957
ARTHUR F. BURNS

ECONOMIC PLANNING IN UNDERDEVELOPED AREAS
• NUMBER TWO • *1958*
EDWARD S. MASON

A PROGRAM FOR MONETARY STABILITY • NUMBER
THREE • *1959*
MILTON FRIEDMAN

THE KEYNESIAN SYSTEM • NUMBER FOUR • *1961*
DAVID MC CORD WRIGHT

THE STRATEGY OF ECONOMIC POLICY • NUMBER FIVE
• *1962*
RAYMOND J. SAULNIER

THE STOCK MARKET AND ECONOMIC EFFICIENCY
• NUMBER SIX • *1965*
WILLIAM J. BAUMOL

TOWARD FULL EMPLOYMENT IN OUR FREE ENTERPRISE ECONOMY

MORRIS A. COPELAND

THE MILLAR LECTURES • NUMBER SEVEN • 1966

FORDHAM UNIVERSITY PRESS • NEW YORK

© FORDHAM UNIVERSITY PRESS • 1966 • NEW YORK
LIBRARY OF CONGRESS CATALOG CARD NUMBER: 66-16972

Foreword

HAVING ATTENDED the lectures delivered by Professor Copeland at Fordham University in October, 1965, it is an academic pleasure and a privilege to be able to peruse them at leisure in their printed form. The irritants of a crowded lecture hall make it difficult to follow a lecture characterized by detailed empirical evidence, close reasoning and careful analysis on the macroeconomic level.

It might be useful to the reader if I present in capsule form, some history in numbers, as a background against which the problem of unemployment and its solution is posed. On the following page will be found a table of the annual percentage figures of the unemployed of the constantly increasing civilian labor force, during the last twenty years.

When these lectures were delivered, in October, 1965, we had a total employment of 73.2 million, with unemployment slightly less than 2.3 million, giving a civilian labor force of 75.5 million. Non-agricultural employment was 68.2 million. Notice that the

v

UNEMPLOYMENT AS A PERCENTAGE
OF THE CIVILIAN LABOR FORCE

1945	1.9	1957	4.3
1946	3.9	1958	6.8
1947	3.9	1959	5.5
1948	3.8	1960	5.6
1949	5.9	1961	6.7
1950	5.3	1962	5.6
1951	3.3	1963	5.7
1952	3.1	1964	5.2
1953	2.9	1965 (Nov.)	4.2
1954	5.6	1965 (Dec.)	4.1
1955	4.4	1966 (Jan.)	4.0
1956	4.2	1966 (Feb.)	3.7

unemployment rate has fallen, at present writing, for six consecutive months, and in February, 1966 was 3.7 percent, the lowest figure in thirteen years.

We have experienced no severe depressions for the last twenty-six years, although there were three relatively minor recessions. (Recessions, for the uninitiate, is a new word in economic terminology, with psychological overtones, used to indicate the difference between a severe and a not-so-severe depression.) Furthermore, we have in the Spring of 1966 completed sixty months of prosperity, growth, increasing Gross National Product, etc., with most economic indicators predicting, in this unpredictable world, another year of upswing prosperity. This is a record breaker in the 175-year history of the business cycle. It has aroused considerable speculation in economic academic circles as to whether we have finally overcome the business cycle or merely dampened the amplitude of the waves.

However, despite this unprecedented maintenance of prosperity, there has persisted a hard core of unemployment. For eight years after World War II, aggregate demand was high, real economic growth was accelerating and by 1953, unemployment was down to what seems, in retrospect, a highly satisfactory minimal percentage. But since 1953, unemployment has been higher at each successive peak. It was 2½ percent in 1953, 4 percent in 1957, 5 percent in 1960. Since 1960 and up to the autumn of 1965, despite four and a half years of prosperity, unemployment never dropped below 5 percent, averaging well above that figure much of the time. This is the problem that Professor Copeland investigates and for which he proposes solutions. As simply as I can state it, and in a highly simplified form, Professor Copeland asks: "How much government action and what kind of government action are requisite and sufficient to adjust the amount of aggregate demand with promptness and precision, to raise it to a full-capacity level and keep it there?" Secondly, "What action is required to iron out the amplitude and frequency of the business-cycle waves, thus reducing cyclical unemployment to some unavoidable minimum?" And finally, "While accomplishing this, is it possible to avoid undesirable inflation?"

It must be admitted, I think, that the current timeliness and the instant urgency of the unemployment problem has been affected by recent developments. The Bureau of Labor Statistics of the Department of Labor reported that, in February, 1966, the seasonally adjusted unemployment rate fell to 3.7 percent of the labor force. Arthur M. Ross, Commissioner of Labor Statistics, predicted, on March 8, 1966, that the rate "will continue down as the year progresses." A front-page *New York Times* headline, March 8, 1966, reports: "President Asks Bold Steps to Avert Labor Shortages. Calls for New Approaches to Problems as Nation's Rate of Unemployment Falls to Lowest Level since '53." The Want-Ad sections of metropolitan newspapers are bulging with pleas for skilled, professional and trained workers. A *Wall Street Journal* front-page headline, March 10, 1966, states: "More Workers Gather Nerve to Switch Jobs as Labor Gets Scarcer." These recent developments, however, do not diminish the ultimate utility and value of this research project. What has happened, can happen and will probably happen again.

Totalitarian states, dictatorships, benevolent and otherwise, are usually not plagued by unemployment problems. The armed forces can sop up some excessive manpower and labor conscription and other forms of *Arbeitsdienst* absorb some more. Political and religious dissidents can be employed in conscription camps. Siberian mines and forests are sometimes available for ethnic minority groups that do not see eye-to-eye with the administration. Any competent economist, with absolute political and administrative power could draw up a blueprint that would guarantee full labor employment. Professor Copeland, however, emphasizes that his proposals are workable under a free enterprise economic system. Quoting Keynes, he believes that we can leave it to "private self-interest . . . to determine what in particular is produced, in what proportion the factors of production will be combined to produce it, and how the value of the final product will be distributed between them."

This full-employment blueprint does, of course, call for considerable government activity, activity which can be classified as economic assistance, intervention, or interference, depending on the point of view. Tax credits, tax bonuses, tax penalties, improvement of existing arrangements, license provisions for attrition, G.N.P. scheduling agency, employer taxes for the support of unemployment compensation, separation-wage requirements, Commodity Stabilization Corporation, and a multitude of other concepts and proposals discussed in the text, will probably not be welcomed with open arms by laissez-faire employers, already overburdened with requests, reports, questionnaires and other forms of governmental red tape. It may be that this is the price we must pay for a planned economic society, a society that does not accept the Catholic socio-economic principle of subsidiarity presented in various papal encyclicals.

Theoretical economics aspires to the status of a science, even an exact science. As a former mentor of mine, at the London School of Economics, Lionel Robbins, now Lord Robbins, used to insist, economics is concerned with what is, not with what ought to be. Moral "oughts," ethical "shoulds" are mere value judgments, scientifically unprovable, and as such, not entitled to any place in scientific economics. Whatever is to be said about this position, and it is at least debatable, applied practical economics is another question. Welfare economics and public finance, for example, inevitably propose solutions to economic problems, expressed in terms of equity, fairness, justice, benefit received, ability to pay, etc. Shades of the medieval Scholastics with their preachments about fair prices, wages and interest rates!

With reference to policy and recommendations for government action, based on scientific, economic analysis, there still remains possible difference of opinion as to what should be done. In conclusion, I point out that Professor Copeland remarks: "Personally, I think we should take such measures, but I will not attempt to press my personal views on you."

JOHN L. SHEA, S.J.
Associate Professor of Economics

Department of Economics
Fordham University
March 15, 1966

Prefatory Note

ON THREE SUCCESSIVE THURSDAYS during October, I had the honor of giving the 1965 Moorhouse I. X. Millar Lectures. This volume, the seventh in the Series, prints those lectures, except for minor changes of wording, exactly as I gave them.

Our free enterprise economy is the most productive economy the world has yet developed, but it is by no means as efficient as it should be. Probably its most serious defect is that much of the time it has operated at a less-than-capacity level. As a result we have produced substantially less than we might have produced. As a result, too, there has been a great deal of suffering on the part of those persons who, though seeking employment, have been unable to find it.

A major part of the unemployment that has characterized the operation of our economy results from a more or less persistent deficiency in the total demand for our Gross National Product. Even at the period of maximum business activity during a business cycle, aggregate demand has ordinarily, in peacetime, been too small to raise production and employment to a capacity level.

A major part of the unemployment we have had is attributable to inadequacies of aggregate demand. But there is what is called frictional unemployment, too. Each year there are some new entrants into the labor force who do not find jobs immediately. Each year, also, there are people whose jobs have ceased to exist because of technological and other changes in our economy; such people may be out of work for some time before they find new jobs. Further, there are always people who have left one job and not yet begun another. And there is seasonal unemployment.

During the six years ending with 1964 on the average more than 5.5 percent of the country's civilian labor force were unemployed. This period included the 1960 business recession, but since February 1961 most of the economy has been enjoying a period of prosperity and expanding business. To explain the high level of unemployment in these years it has been suggested that recent changes in the structure of our economy have increased the amount of frictional unemployment that could not be eliminated by raising aggregate demand to a full-capacity level. An important current question is, how much frictional unemployment is unavoidable under our free enterprise system?

It is true our economy did a good deal better in 1965 than it had been doing in the six preceding years. Also we have made significant if modest progress in dealing with problems of less-than-capacity operation. But certainly we are not yet able and ready to manage our affairs so as to iron out the business cycle and to maintain continuously a capacity-level of operation.

There are, indeed, some economists today who seem to think the knowledge we have recently acquired has provided a complete solution of the problems of less-than-capacity operation, that we now know how to steer our economy between the Scylla of inflation and the Charybdis of depression. But there are others who think that what can be done about those problems within the framework of our free enterprise system is rather limited. I believe the truth lies somewhere between these two positions. For a number of years I have been wanting to take the time to develop my ideas on what I would consider an adequate full-capacity employment program. When Fordham University invited me to give the 1965 Millar Lectures I was delighted. It was both a privilege and a long-wished-for opportunity. I am deeply grateful to Fordham University.

The ideas I offer here are necessarily tentative. No doubt, among my readers there will be those who see difficulties in my proposals that I have not yet seen. I only hope that those who do will be stimulated to offer proposals of their own.

I have sought to put together a rounded full-capacity employment program. Several of the parts of the program I offer are, as my lectures made clear, measures proposed by others.

For helpful comments on and criticism of the drafts of my lectures I am deeply grateful to two of my former colleagues at Cornell University, Alfred E. Kahn and George H. Hildebrand. And I want particularly here to express my warm appreciation to Rev. William T. Hogan, S.J., who worked out the arrangements for the lectures. He made my visits to Fordham University not only very convenient for me but also very enjoyable occasions.

MORRIS A. COPELAND

University of Missouri,
Columbia, Mo.

Table of Contents

Foreword by John L. Shea, S.J. v

Prefatory Note xi

Chapter One
How Much Frictional Unemployment Is Unavoidable? . 1

Chapter Two
Ironing Out the Business Cycle 28

Chapter Three
An Adequate Aggregate Employment Program . . . 53

Index 78

Chapter One

How Much Frictional Unemployment Is Unavoidable?

IN 1933, PRACTICALLY ONE-FOURTH of the members of our civilian labor force were unemployed. And recovery from this depression level was slow and far from vigorous. Even in 1941, despite the impetus that war preparedness had been giving the economy, the unemployment figure was 9.9 percent.[1]

Of course, during the latter part of World War II practically everyone who wanted employment was able to find it. Quite naturally, though, as the war drew to a close there was wide-

[1] *Economic Report of the President,* January, 1965, p. 214.

1

spread concern about the possibility of severe postwar unemployment. In the summer of 1945, a government document known as the V-J Day Forecast was issued. It predicted that some 13 percent of the labor force would be unemployed during the second quarter of 1946.[2]

At about this time, too, various proposals were advanced that were aimed at keeping our economy operating continuously at a full-capacity level. These proposals, while operating within the framework of our free enterprise type of organization, were intended to give us a planned economy so far as the level of G.N.P. was concerned. But the V-J Day Forecast proved to be something of a false alarm. During the second quarter of 1946 the unemployment figure was only about 4 percent, and during 1947 and 1948, the average was just under 4 percent. The prompt attainment of a high peace-time level of aggregate demand eliminated much of the concern about the possibility of excessive postwar unemployment, and the erroneous V-J Day Forecast helped to discourage doing very much about such a possibility. The Employment Act of 1946, instead of moving definitely in the direction of aggregate economic planning as some of its sponsors had intended, merely established a Council of Economic Advisors whose functions were purely recommendatory, and made full employment an acknowledged objective of federal policy.

To the questions what is full employment? and how much unemployment is unavoidable under a free enterprise system such as ours, various answers have been offered. Theodore Yntema, in one of the earliest discussions of the subject, said 2 to 5 per-

[2] Michael Sapir, "Review of Economic Forecasts for the Transition Period," in *Studies in Income and Wealth*, XI, National Bureau of Economic Research.

cent.[3] Lord Beveridge at about the same time said 2 percent.[4] A widely accepted figure in 1946, when the Employment Act was passed, was 3 percent. But now that we have had seven successive years with unemployment at or above the 5 percent level there has been a tendency to think in terms of a somewhat higher minimum.

If there have been differences of opinion as to how big the unavoidable minimum really is, there is quite general agreement as to why it cannot be zero. There are four kinds of unemployment that must always be present in a free enterprise economy if its labor market is to function properly. First, there must always be some people who are in process of changing jobs, some who have left one job and not yet started on another. Or, to state the matter in terms of significance for economic efficiency, the labor market should never be so tight that workers have no incentive to be on their toes. There must always be some between-job unemployment. Second, there must always be some persons who have lost their jobs because, as a result of technological or other changes, the jobs have ceased to exist. It may take some time for such persons to find new employment. Probably there must always be some so-called structural unemployment. Third, there will always be people who have just entered the labor force, and inevitably some of these people will not find jobs immediately. There must be some new-job-seeker unemployment. And fourth, some seasonal unemployment seems unavoidable in an economy such as ours.

Each of these four types of unemployment—we may use the

[3] " 'Full' Employment in a Private Enterprise System," *American Economic Review*, March Supplement, 1944, pp. 197 ff.

[4] William H. Beveridge, *Full Employment in a Free Society* (New York, 1944).

term frictional unemployment to cover all four—helps to explain why full employment cannot mean the employment of everyone who is able and willing to work. If frictional unemployment could be sharply distinguished from other unemployment—unemployment that is due to an inadequate level of aggregate demand—it might still be difficult to determine whether the minimum unavoidable figure is 2 percent or 5 percent of the civilian labor force. But, in fact, the line between the two kinds of unemployment is a hazy one. Despite all the statistical information we have available today, the amount of frictional unemployment cannot be at all precisely determined.

We do, however, have some information about frictional unemployment in 1957. For that year the Bureau of Labor Statistics made a special analysis of labor force data for the Joint Economic Committee to determine, as far as possible, the extent of frictional unemployment.[5] On the basis of this study the following fractional unemployment rates—i.e., ratios to the total civilian labor force—can readily be computed:

Unemployment rate due to voluntary job changes	.43%
Unemployment rate identified as long-term, due to structural changes	.43%
Unemployment rate due to persons entering the labor market	.86%
Unemployment rate identified as seasonal	.86%
Unemployment rate not identified by type	1.72%
The overall unemployment rate	4.30%

Thus the Bureau identified sixty percent of the unemployment during 1957 as frictional. It did not attempt to classify the

[5] Bureau of Labor Statistics, *The Extent and Nature of Frictional Unemployment,* Joint Economic Committee Study Paper No. 6, 86th Congress, 1st Session.

remaining forty percent except to note that the percentage of unemployment identified as seasonal was too small. Probably the unemployment rate for voluntary job changers reflected most but by no means all between-job unemployment. And presumably the structural rate as well as the seasonal rate is understated in these figures. But the part of unemployment attributable to persons entering the labor force included not only first-job-seekers; it included also persons who had left the labor force for a time and then re-entered it. In any event, not all of the 4.3 percent was merely frictional. For certainly the G.N.P. did not reach a capacity level during the year. In fact, the percentage of capacity utilized seems to have been less than in 1956.[6]

These comments on the 1957 situation make it seem reasonable to say that the unavoidable minimum amount of frictional unemployment is more likely to be 3 percent than 4 percent of the civilian labor force. Nonetheless, for some time now it has been contended that our economy has been undergoing a secular change, a change making for a higher minimum figure. Let us consider this contention for a moment. One form of it assumes that the gradual increase in the educational and training requirements for employment that technological progress entails has outstripped the improvement that has taken place in our labor force. Consequently, the argument runs, an increasing proportion of the members of our labor force are unable to find employment because they lack the education and training that would be necessary to make it profitable to employ them. Various facts have been cited in support of this contention. For one thing, it is pointed out that the unemployment rate for persons 14 to 19 years of age has increased sharply. It was 10.8 percent

[6] See *Economic Report of the President,* January, 1962, p. 55. *Ibid,* January, 1963, p. 27.

in 1957, 14.7 percent in 1964.[7] For another, the unemployment rate tends to vary negatively with educational attainment. Of all males 18 years of age and over, 5.2 percent were unemployed in 1964. For those who had completed less than eight years of schooling the unemployment rate was 8.4 percent; for those who had completed 16 years or more, only 1.5 percent.[8] Furthermore, there are marked differences in the unemployment rates for different occupations. For experienced members of the labor force the overall average rate was 4.4 percent in 1964. For experienced blue-collar workers, it was 6.3 percent; for white-collar workers, 2.6 percent; for others, chiefly service employees, it was 4.9 percent.[9]

But I do not think these figures prove that the necessary minimum frictional unemployment rate has been gradually increasing. It should be agreed today that most of the time the physical volume of our national product varies from quarter to quarter in response to changes in aggregate demand, and that the importance of supply conditions is that they set an upper limit for this volume. An increase in the size of our labor force, or in its efficiency, would not be sufficient alone to bring about an increase in our national output. Nor would an increase in the stock of business plant and business equipment alone be sufficient. If there is to be an increase in output, the labor force must be capable of producing it; likewise, the stock of plant and equipment must be capable of producing it. But capacity alone is not enough; there must also be an appropriate increase in aggregate demand.

The pertinence of these statements to the question in hand

---

[7] *Economic Report of the President*, January, 1965, p. 217.
[8] *Ibid.*, p. 126.
[9] *Monthly Labor Review*, April, 1965, pp. 389–90.

should be clear. To contend that the high level of unemployment that has prevailed during the past seven years is due in whole or in part to deficiencies in the education and training of a significant number of those who have been unemployed is to contend that the number of unemployed would have been significantly less, if the unemployed had been somewhat better educated and better trained. In other words, the contention is equivalent to asserting that, if the productive capacity of our labor force had been larger, our G.N.P. would have been larger. The contention confuses what may be called a permissive condition for a production increase with a sufficient condition. The sufficient condition would be an increase in aggregate demand. I think the potential increase in the productive capacity of the labor force through education and training should be called a permissive condition for a G.N.P. increase. As things stand—as long as there is excess capacity—such a change in the labor force would be neither a sufficient nor a necessary condition. It seems reasonable to say that deficiencies in the qualifications of the unskilled part of the labor force play a major role in determining who is to be unemployed, when the economy operates at less than capacity, but that these deficiencies play no significant part in determining the level at which the economy operates.

But there is another form of the contention that our economy has been changing in a way that has increased the minimum percentage of the labor force that must inevitably be unemployed. This form emphasizes primarily the rate at which jobs have gone out of existence, rather than deficiencies in education and training. The most difficult type of frictional unemployment to deal with when one attempts to say how much unemployment is unavoidable is structural unemployment, unemployment that results when a job ceases to exist. A job may come to an end because of automation or some other technological innovation. But it may come to an end in other ways too. The employer may move away, or he may go out of business.

When a job terminates, the worker becomes unemployed regardless of his education and training. But his qualifications for other employment help to determine his mobility and the duration of his unemployment. The volume of structural unemployment at any time depends partly on the number of recent job terminations, partly on the degree of mobility—both interoccupational and geographical—that those persons whose jobs have recently ceased to exist must possess if they are to get other jobs, and partly on the degree of mobility that these persons do in fact possess. But this is not quite all. The volume of structural unemployment at any time depends also—as does the volume of other frictional unemployment—on the level of aggregate demand. That is, as I have already noted, the line between frictional unemployment and inadequate-aggregate-demand unemployment cannot be drawn sharply. Decrease aggregate demand, and you increase what seems to be frictional unemployment. Our immediate concern, however, is not with this aspect of the situation, but with the rate at which people have been becoming structurally unemployed and with the mobility they possess and the mobility required of them. The volume of structural unemployment may have increased during the past several years either because so many jobs have ceased to exist or because it has taken so long to make the adjustments, in occupation and in place of residence, required of those who have become structurally unemployed. One set of facts appears to support the hypothesis that the high unemployment rate that has prevailed during the past seven years is, in part at least, a result either of the increased number of persons whose jobs have ceased to exist, or of the increased difficulty in the occupational and residential adjustments these persons have had to make. During the decade ending with the year 1957, the average number of unemployed persons was 2.75 million. Only 7.8 percent of them were persons who had been unemployed for more than 26 weeks. During the 7-year period ending with 1964, the average number of unemployed persons was 4.19 million; 14.1 percent of them were identified as having been unemployed for more than 26 weeks.[10] It seems reasonable to interpret this sharp step-up as reflecting in considerable part an increase in structural unemployment. And, presumably, the larger volume of structural unemployment in this recent period is due to a combination of circumstances: to more job terminations, to more difficulties for those who became structurally unemployed in making the necessary occupational and residential adjustments, and to an inadequate level of aggregate demand.

Can we conclude from the increase in long-term unemployment that the minimum number of people that must be unemployed when the economy is operating at capacity is now, say, 4 percent rather than 3 percent of our civilian labor force? I do not think this follows. It is true that the minimum unemployment level has often been considered to be the level to which unemployment would be reduced if aggregate demand were to be increased enough to raise our G.N.P. to the capacity level. On this view, it would be a possible conclusion. But there are two objections to this way of defining the minimum unemployment level.

One of them is suggested by the question: What is it that determines the capacity level of our G.N.P.? In 1944, when the unemployment rate was down to 1.2 percent of our civilian labor force, the size and efficiency of that force was quite possibly the main determining factor. But in 1941, when 9.9 percent of the

[10] See *Economic Report of the President,* January, 1965, p. 218.

labor force was unemployed, the main factor limiting our national output was probably the capacity of our plant and equipment. The minimum unavoidable level of unemployment should surely be defined in a way that would rule out the possibility of an unemployment situation like that of 1941.

But that is perhaps a remote possibility. A far more serious objection to defining the minimum unemployment level as the level to which unemployment would be reduced by raising G.N.P. to capacity rate is that it takes the existing arrangements that are responsible for frictional unemployment for granted. But certainly various things can be done to reduce frictional unemployment by improving those arrangements. It is not my present purpose to consider in detail what might be done along these lines. A brief comment on each type of frictional unemployment should serve to indicate that there are a number of steps that might be taken.

Seasonal unemployment is due to several factors, among them weather conditions, holiday sales peaks, and model change-overs. But not a few businesses have found it worth-while to dovetail different operations so as to improve their employment load factors. Also, collective bargaining agreements that call for some form of annual wage push in this direction. And it has been suggested that employer taxes for the support of unemployment compensation might well be varied so as to give employers a more definite incentive to iron out their seasonal variations. Since this is an aspect of unemployment that employers can, to some extent control, a merit rating system that concentrated on seasonal unemployment might well have a substantial effect.

In the average month during 1964, 16 percent of the 3.9 million unemployed persons were first-job seekers. Since the early 1950s, the proportion of total unemployment accounted for by these new members of the labor force had more than doubled.[11] But our present concern is with the earlier level. Was it really a minimum? Or could steps have been taken to reduce it? Improvements in vocational guidance, as well as a strengthening of state employment services, are measures that naturally suggest themselves. But there may well be a need of making first-job seekers more attractive to employers. One possibility is providing better education and training for persons before they enter the labor force. Another possibility is a provision for a special new-worker-learner minimum wage rate that would be applicable to young persons for a limited number of months. Still another is that the government might arrange to pay part of the cost private employers incur in connection with the in-service training of new employees.

A certain amount of between-job unemployment is needed to make our free enterprise economy operate properly. Employees want the opportunity to better themselves by changing jobs. Employers need some opportunity to dismiss for cause, whether or not the industry is unionized. And some unemployment is surely needed to give workers an incentive to do their work well. But we would not be justified in assuming that between-job unemployment was at a minimum level in 1957, that the between-job rate could not be reduced below, say, one-half of one percent. The amount of this type of unemployment depends partly on its average duration, partly on the frequency of job changes, i.e., on the rate of labor turnover. Strengthening state employment services would help to cut down the minimum unavoidable amount of between-job unemployment by shortening the average time between jobs.

The report cited above, covering the year 1957, gives labor

[11] *Monthly Labor Review*, April, 1965, p. 388.

turnover information that relates job changes to unemployment. According to this report, 11.6 million persons who had been unemployed found employment during the year, and about 6.6 million who had been employed became unemployed.[12] The report also indicates that 32.6 million persons who entered the labor force during the year were promptly employed,[13] and one can surmise from this report that a somewhat larger number of persons that had been employed withdrew from the labor force. But the facts that bear most directly on the amount of unemployment are those relating to the changes between the status of being employed and that of being unemployed. Evidently, such job status changes that involved unemployment were sufficiently numerous in 1957 to be an important factor in the amount of frictional unemployment. If a material reduction in the number of such changes can be effected, it should mean a material reduction in the amount of frictional unemployment that would be unavoidable if we had an adequate level of aggregate demand. A comparison of the unemployment figures for first-job seekers, about 620 thousand in 1964, and those for persons 14–19 years of age, about 960 thousand, makes it clear that between-job unemployment is a major factor for these younger members of the labor force.[14] Many teenagers get their first employment experience in jobs for which they are not well suited. Improved arrangements for vocational guidance might significantly reduce

[12] Report by the Bureau of Labor Statistics, Joint Economic Committee Study Paper No. 6, 86th Congress, 1st Session, Tables II-1 and II-2. There are regular monthly reports on the labor turnover of employees in the manufacturing and coal and metal mining industries, but these do not give us details on changes from being employed to being unemployed and vice versa.

[13] *Ibid.*, Table II-2. This figure, no doubt, includes a great many re-entrants.

[14] See the *Economic Report of the President,* January, 1965, p. 216.

teenage unemployment. But job-changing must be a major factor for other categories of workers too. We do not know how much employers could do to make job changes less frequent, but there is reason to believe they could make a significant contribution in this respect. A separation wage requirement might give them an effective incentive to do so.

What can be done to reduce the minimum unavoidable amount of structural unemployment is a particularly difficult question. In general, it seems desirable not only to permit, but also to encourage changes in the structure of our economy that may mean increases in its efficiency, not only to permit but also to encourage improvements in technological processes and in industry locations, as well as the replacement of less by more efficient business managements. Quite commonly such structural changes have meant that jobs have ceased to exist and that those who held these jobs have suffered structural unemployment and loss of earning power. One not entirely satisfactory way of avoiding this kind of development is through provisions for attrition. When a prospective structural change threatens the abolition of a particular job, the job may be continued in existence until the incumbent reaches the retirement age.

It seems reasonable to hold that structural changes that make for economic efficiency should not be permitted to take place in ways that substantially damage workers' earning power when workers have no way to recover the damages they suffer. A provision for attrition applicable to a particular job can prevent a large part of the damages that might otherwise be inflicted. If it not only maintains the job, but also provides for reasonable pay increases during the worker's working life, his interests may be considered reasonably well cared for. However, it is by no means clear that job maintenance is the best solution for younger workers. Provision for money damages covering loss of earnings during a limited period and for appropriate job training might well be preferable.

But the major part of the present problem of how to deal with structural-change unemployment arises because it has thus far been dealt with mainly through collective bargaining agreements. This means, for one thing, that there are substantial areas of employment where little or nothing has been done about structural-change unemployment. Besides, it means various job maintenance arrangements that are aimed at keeping what should be obsolete jobs in existence for a more or less indefinite period, arrangements that effectively hamper making changes in the structure of our economy that would improve its efficiency.

Admittedly the situation is a difficult one. Despite the fact that action by the federal government to remedy it would almost certainly have to overcome strong trade union opposition, I venture to urge that some federal action is called for. Just what form that action could best take is by no means clear. To indicate the kind of help and guidance I think the government should provide, I will very tentatively mention three possibilities: 1) The government could undertake to license provisions for attrition, issuing to the employer involved a separate license for each job covered, and it could regulate the terms under which such licenses would be issued; 2) The government could subsidize attrition provision licenses. It is reasonable that the government should assume some part of the financial burden such provisions entail. The subsidy might well be large enough to extend considerably the areas of employment covered by attrition provisions; 3) A tax could probably be devised that would apply to the maintenance of obsolescent jobs not covered by attrition provision licenses. A very small payroll tax might be sufficient to discourage establishing new provisions for this kind of job maintenance. It might help to make arrangements along these lines acceptable if licenses covering most job maintenance provisions in existence at the time of inaugurating the licensing were to be granted on liberal terms. It might help, also, if the tax were applied only to those job maintenance provisions established after the inauguration of the tax, for which no licenses had been obtained.

These three suggestions, if they could be adopted, might do something to decrease the amount of structural unemployment. But their main purpose is to reduce the extent to which job maintenance arrangements have come to hamper economic progress. At least so long as we continue to have an inadequate level of aggregate demand, there will be problems of relief for distressed areas and for special groups. Various made-work measures have been taken to provide relief, among them the Appalachia program and the Job Corps. It is probable that still others will be taken before very long. It seems to me, however, that if we were to establish and maintain a capacity level of aggregate demand, we should be able to deal with the problem of structural unemployment that is not avoided through reasonably justifiable job maintenance provisions entirely by arrangements for earnings-loss compensation and by retraining. Made-work measures for relief should be regarded as necessary temporary expedients.

It has usually been assumed that there are only the four kinds of frictional unemployment thus far commented on. But discussions of the recent high level of unemployment suggest that there may be a fifth; a kind of unemployment that is concentrated in particular categories of workers for whom, at the current wage rates, supply is substantially greater than demand.[15]

[15] For a suggestion along these lines see George H. Hildebrand, *Some Alternative Views of the Current Unemployment Problem in the U. S.* (This is in process of publication by the International Labor Office.)

Let us call this worker-type overpricing-unemployment. It should, I think, be agreed that this is a type of unemployment that, like the other four frictional types, might well exist if aggregate demand were at a full capacity level. It should probably be agreed, too, that even if demand stayed at the capacity level for some time, it might continue to be unprofitable to employ these workers, unless product prices increased considerably. However, so long as we have a substantial deficiency in aggregate demand, it is difficult to say whether in fact there is any worker-type overpricing-unemployment. And, in any case, it seems unlikely that worker overpricing explains more than a small part of the marked increase in unemployment that has characterized the last several years.

These somewhat sketchy comments on the various forms of frictional unemployment and possible measures to decrease each of the first four should make it clear that we cannot define the unavoidable minimum figure for unemployment as the figure to which it would be reduced if aggregate demand were raised to a capacity level. We must also take account of what can be done about the present arrangements that help to determine how much frictional unemployment there would be with aggregate demand raised to this level.

In a way we have been assuming that all of the unemployment that is due to the inadequacy of aggregate demand is avoidable. But is it? Can we expect in a free enterprise economy like ours to be able to raise aggregate demand to a capacity level, and keep it there? Keynes clearly thought so. He thought the central government could "succeed in establishing an aggregate volume of output corresponding to full employment." He thought the government should establish such a volume of output and that at the same time it could and should allow "private self-interest . . . [to] determine what in particular is produced, in what

proportions the factors of production will be combined to produce it, and how the value of the final product will be distributed
between them." [16] Was Keynes right about the compatibility of
full employment and free enterprise? If so, we must face the
question: what government actions does establishing an adequate aggregate volume of output call for?

But today many economists have views on government policy
that disagree with Keynes. Let us consider briefly three such
views. First, there are those who hold that Keynes's way of
providing full employment is unnecessarily radical, and that it
would be more in accord with our free enterprise tradition to
eliminate excess-capacity unemployment by decreasing the size
of the labor force. Second, there are those who think that, since
business cycles now involve only minor recessions, the general
policy we have been following should be continued. And third,
there are those who emphasize the difficulties of reconciling the
full employment objective with the objective of avoiding inflation and who insist that we must avoid inflation if we are to keep
our free enterprise system.

The size of the labor force might be reduced in various ways.
For our present purpose it may suffice to note three: 1) Steps
can be taken—and some have been taken—to decrease the
length of the working week or the work year; 2) young people
might be kept in school longer; and 3) old people might be
retired earlier. Each of these ways of reducing the labor supply
may be thought of as a possible means of remedying a continuing, secular deficiency in aggregate demand. Probably, too,
many people will consider each of them less radical than increasing aggregate demand by going in for deficit financing to step

[16] John Maynard Keynes, *The General Theory of Employment, Interest and Money* (New York: Harcourt, Brace and Company, 1936), pp.
378–79.

up government expenditures or to cut taxes. One difficulty with this approach is that it is not sufficiently flexible. At any rate, the proposals for keeping young people in school longer and for earlier retirement are not. To deal with unemployment at all fully by changing the size of the labor force, it would be necessary to adjust the size at least annually and to have the adjustments take effect promptly. It would be theoretically possible to adjust the work year in this way.[17] The other two ways of changing the size of the labor force could not deal very well with year to year fluctuations in aggregate demand.

But the real objection to this approach, to my mind, is not its lack of flexibility. The length of the work year probably could, in theory, be decreased and increased so that year-to-year fluctuations in the capacity of the labor force would match the fluctuations in aggregate demand. The real objection is that what the length of the working life should be and what the length of the work year should be are questions that ought to be decided on their own merits. If we decide to keep young people in school longer, it should be because we think more schooling is desirable. Any decision about retirement of older persons should be made both with reference to the way in which their effectiveness as workers diminishes with age and in view of their need for activities that interest them. Decisions regarding the length of the work-year should take account of the desirability of additional leisure and the feasibility of providing it at our present stage of economic development. On none of these questions is the level of aggregate demand at any particular time a pertinent consideration.

So much for proposals to eliminate unemployment by reduc-

[17] See for example Benjamin Graham, *The Flexible Work-Year*, The Center for the Study of Democratic Institutions (Santa Barbara, Cal., 1964).

ing the size of the labor force. Next, as to the policy regarding unemployment that we have been following. That policy reflects both the changes that have been made or that have taken place in our economy in the last 30 or 40 years and the fact that, since Keynes, we have had a branch of economic theorizing known as macro-economics. There have been three principal kinds of changes in our economy. First, various measures were taken during the 1930s that greatly strengthened the economy's financial structure. Second, the relative size of the government component of aggregate demand has substantially increased. It was 8.1 percent of total G.N.P. in 1929; 20.5 percent in 1964. Third, federal government receipts and expenditures have come to behave in a way that tends appreciably to dampen cyclical fluctuations in business activity; we now have what has been called a built-in fiscal countercycle. A good many economists have come to believe that because of these changes the business cycle has become permanently milder. Perhaps it is fair to remind those who do so, of a possible historical parallel. During the period of high prosperity that preceded the stock market crash in 1929, two of the then leading students of business cycles made pronouncements to the effect that, in their opinions, the cycle had become permanently milder. Possibly those who think this way today have been too much impressed by the prosperous times that, on the whole, have prevailed since World War II. But I suspect, also, that they may have a somewhat exaggerated idea of how much we have learned since the 1920s. A large part of what we now know about the impacts of fiscal and monetary policy on the volume of business activity was known before the term "macro-economics" was introduced.

But what has been our policy in regard to full employment since the Employment Act of 1946 made it an official policy objective? It can be quite briefly summarized. It has been to rely primarily on our built-in fiscal countercycle and on Federal Reserve monetary and credit policy so far as minor business cycles are concerned, and to take important further actions to promote full employment only when specific situations seem to call for them. The high level of unemployment during the past seven years has been recognized as such a situation, but the actions taken can hardly be considered either particularly prompt or entirely adequate. And while the unemployment percentage has decreased considerably in recent months, it remains to be seen whether an increase in this percentage that many had expected will not shortly materialize.

The policy we have been following means tolerating a considerable amount of unemployment. I think it means also gambling that there will never be another major contraction of business activity. It is true the policy has been defended on the basis that we now know enough about macro-economics so that we can control the level at which our economy operates, and that we would not again permit any really large decrease in it. But does the policy we have been following give any assurance on this point? The answer seems to be no. We do not decide what to do about a major business contraction until we get into one. That would mean waiting during a cyclical downswing until it became evident that it was really a major one, and then waiting longer still for the Congress to frame and enact appropriate legislation and to appropriate the money to implement it. During the interval between the start of the downswing and the time when the new measures to deal with it could begin to get effectively under way a very substantial decrease in G.N.P. might well have taken place and the downswing might have gained enough momentum to make converting it into an upswing extremely difficult.

Still you may be wondering whether there is much chance

of another major contraction in business activity. The three types of change in our economy I have noted all tend to moderate the cycle, and countercyclical Federal Reserve policy also exerts an influence in this direction. But it is well not to overstate the influence that the Federal Reserve can exert or the extent of the changes in our economy. The Federal Reserve could not be expected to stop a cyclical downswing or to start an upswing. And once a downswing gets underway the decrease in each decreasing component of aggregate demand can still be counted on to encourage additional decreases in other components. Moreover, it continues to be true that the amount of aggregate demand is not centrally planned. Each party that purchases a part of our national product remains free to decide to decrease his purchases. Nothing has been done to prevent such decreases in the areas that have played the largest parts in past peacetime contractions of aggregate demand. Nothing has been done to prevent decreased purchases of business equipment and of consumers' durable goods, or decreases in the volume of construction contracts.

These various points can be restated as a single point. Our economy is still subject to business cycles. But we cannot adequately appraise the possibilities of another major business contraction if we consider the United States as if it were an isolated economy. In the 1929–33 contraction most of the free world participated and its severity was due in large part to this fact. During the past 30-odd years more and more of the world's production has come to be production for a market. That development means that a major cyclical contraction of business activity would almost inevitably be one in which many countries would participate. I think it also makes such a cyclical downswing rather more likely. It does not seem very wise to continue to follow a policy that not only accepts a substantial amount of unemployment as a necessary evil but also, in effect, assumes the impossibility of a major world-wide contraction of business activity.

But before we consider what kinds of government action would be needed to establish and maintain an adequate level of aggregate demand, we must examine the contention that such a level would involve extremely dangerous inflationary pressures. Inflation is a threat to the continued existence of our free enterprise type of economic organization, because we may find price and wage controls necessary to keep it within bounds. We did during both World Wars. Certainly to resort to such controls on a permanent peacetime basis would involve a serious curtailment of freedom of contract.

Temporary wartime price and wage controls were needed because increased government expenditures raised aggregate demand to levels that exceeded the economy's production capacity. The wartime experience has been cited as proving that it would be possible through fiscal policy to raise peacetime aggregate demand to a full-capacity level and to keep it there. I think it proves this. And I think it proves also that, if we are to have a continuing, full-capacity level of employment and at the same time to avoid ever overtaxing the economy's capacity to produce, we must find ways to make very prompt and very precise adjustments in the amount of aggregate demand. For a workable full employment program prompt and precise adjustments would be essential, for an excessive amount of aggregate demand would presumably not need to be much greater than a full-capacity amount.

But some of those who contend that a full-capacity employment program would involve dangerous inflationary pressures claim that there might be such pressures even when there is a good deal of unemployment. Let us consider this claim.

But first let us recognize that some forces making for price increases have been with us pretty continuously ever since World War II. Even during the past seven or eight years we have had what is called creeping inflation, in spite of the high unemployment rate that has prevailed. It is true that the prices farmers received for livestock products—particularly poultry and eggs—declined during this period. But most other prices rose. The G.N.P. implicit price index increased from 97.5 in 1957 to 110.7 in the second quarter of 1965.[18] This kind of inflation has caused some inequities certainly, but we do not think it means any call for general price and wage controls.

As business volume increases during the upswing phase of a business cycle there has commonly been a more or less general increase in prices. If aggregate demand rises sufficiently to tax the economy's production capacity, the price increase becomes sharp. But the increase in prices during a cyclical upswing has commonly been only in part a result of demand-pull; cost-push has usually been involved, too. Those who claim that there may be dangerous inflationary pressures even when there is a good deal of unemployment, presumably believe that during a cyclical upswing a sharp price increase could occur before the unemployment rate has fallen to a 2 or 3 percent level, perhaps even before it has fallen to a 4 percent level.[19] This is alleged to be the case, as I understand it, because recent changes in the structure of our economy have so greatly strengthened cost-push tendencies.

[18] See *Survey of Current Business,* August, 1965, pp. 52, S1, and S2. 1958 = 100 per cent.

[19] An hypothesis along these lines was suggested by Paul A. Samuelson and Robert M. Solow in 1959 on the basis of the record at that time. See their "Analytical Aspects of Anti-Inflation Policy," *American Economic Review,* May, 1960, pp. 177–94.

The claim we are here concerned with then is that with a high enough level of aggregate demand to reduce the unemployment percentage to, say, 3 percent, prices and wages would increase at a rate that would be more rapid than we would be willing to tolerate. The claim assumes a particular pattern of relationship between the percentage of the labor force that is unemployed and the rate of price increase. It assumes that when the unemployment percentage is reduced to some such figure as 4 percent, prices and wages will increase sharply. For our present economy this is a possible hypothesis certainly. But equally certain is the fact that it is not an established hypothesis. The time-span to which it applies is still far too short for much exploration of it.

Personally I am extremely sceptical about it. I agree that cost-push tendencies are considerably stronger today than they were in the 1920's or even in the period, 1898–1913. But I doubt the particular unemployment-percentage price-increase pattern it assumes.

Fortunately for purposes of developing a full-capacity employment program we do not need to determine whether there is this kind of a pattern. We do need to assume that the program will be such as to provide for prompt and precise adjustments of the amount of aggregate demand. We need to assume also that instead of the present vague policy of avoiding dangerously inflationary pressures, there will be a definite, established rule regarding the maximum rate of price increase that will be permitted, and that the amount of aggregate demand will be continuously adjusted so as to be as large as possible consistently with this price increase rule.

On these assumptions how would the level of aggregate demand be adjusted? And what difference would it make whether the hypothesis about the pattern between unemployment and price increases about which I am sceptical is correct? The answer to the first question should be clear. So long as the last observed price increase was permissible under the maximum rate increase rule, the next adjustment would be toward a demand increase. But an observed price increase larger than that permitted by the rule would be immediately followed by a downward aggregate demand adjustment. If, then, the hypothesis I question should turn out to be correct and the minimum permissible unemployment percentage should turn out to be, say, 4 percent, the actual percentage would fluctuate around and close to 4 percent. But I think a 4 percent figure assumes not only the correctness of the hypothesis I question, it assumes also that not much is done to reduce the unavoidable minimum amount of frictional unemployment. If I am right, the actual unemployment percentage might average rather less than 3 percent. In either case we would accept the maximum permissible price increase rule as defining what we mean by a full-capacity level of aggregate demand.

A full capacity employment program along these lines, then, would mean that we would continue to have creeping inflation; quite possibly the rate of price increase would be appreciably higher than it has been recently. But we can surely assume that the inflation would be tolerable in the sense that it would not call for price and wage controls. However, as I say, creeping inflation causes inequities. If it were accelerated, the inequities would be more serious. And if we wanted to do something about them, we could do what Alfred Marshall long ago suggested.[20] It involves no restrictions on freedom of enterprise. We could put so-called escalator clauses in long-term contracts—in contracts for bonds and mortgages and in life insurance policies.

[20] See Alfred Marshall, *Official Papers* (London, 1927), pp. 10–31. He had first made his suggestion in 1885. Apparently others had made a proposal along these lines somewhat earlier.

The two chapters that follow will be concerned with the kinds of government action that would be needed to adjust the amount of aggregate demand with the requisite promptness and precision and to raise it to a full-capacity level and keep it there. Let me anticipate them to this extent. Assuming them in operation, let me summarize my answer to the question: how much unemployment is unavoidable under our free enterprise type of economic organization? I have been using and will now use the most commonly cited measure of unemployment. It is not the best measure today available, but it serves the present purpose. If we can largely iron out the business cycle and if we can eliminate any secular deficiency in aggregate demand, as I believe we can, and if I am right about the relation between unemployment and price increase rates, the minimum unavoidable amount of non-frictional unemployment should certainly be somewhat less than one-half of one percent of the civilian labor force. If I am wrong it might be somewhat more; I will not try to say how much more. As for frictional unemployment no valid reason has been proposed for thinking that structural changes in our economy have more than very slightly increased the unavoidable minimum. For 1953, the average unemployment rate—frictional plus nonfrictional—was 2.9 percent. Surely, if appropriate steps are taken to reduce frictional unemployment, the unavoidable minimum frictional rate should be somewhat less than 2.5 percent.

The analysis of frictional unemployment on which this conclusion is based has been concerned with what could be done to reduce it. I have not attempted to argue that what could be done should be done. That is my personal view, but I seek to persuade you only that there are various measures that would materially decrease frictional unemployment, not that such measures are desirable as matters of public policy. In the two chapters that follow, my approach to the subject of a capacity level of employment will be similar. I shall consider various measures that could be taken to raise employment to a capacity level and keep it there, measures that in combination should be sufficient to achieve that objective. It is my personal view that we should take such measures, but I shall not attempt to press my personal view on you. I do hope to convince you that a stable, full-capacity level of employment is feasible under our free enterprise type of economic organization.

Chapter Two

Ironing Out the Business Cycle

IN THE FIRST CHAPTER we examined the reasons why there is a minimum amount of frictional unemployment that is unavoidable under a free enterprise type of economic organization.

For perhaps two centuries now our economy has been subject to business cycles—alternating periods of expansion and contraction in the level of production and employment and in the dollar volume of business activity. And even at the cyclical peaks of activity there have quite commonly been some excess productive capacity in our economy and some unemployment due to the less-than-capacity level of operation. We need at this time to face the question: are business cycles and less-than-

28

capacity operation unavoidable under our type of economic organization?

This is a major question in macro-economics. As a first step toward answering it, let us note the basic macro-economic proposition: the level of national production is determined by aggregate demand. Since, thanks to Keynes, there has been a good deal of confusion on this point, let us be very explicit.[1] The level of national production is not determined as an equilibrium adjustment between aggregate supply and aggregate demand. Supply conditions fix the productive capacity of the economy; demand conditions determine the level of production and the percentage of capacity that is utilized.

Let us, then, restate our question about the possibility of avoiding business cycles and less-than-capacity operation under our free enterprise system. Can we find ways to raise aggregate demand to a capacity level and keep it there? Can we find ways that would nonetheless leave it to "private self-interest . . . [to] determine what in particular is produced, in what proportions the factors of production will be combined to produce it, and how the value of the final product will be distributed between them"?

It will be convenient to assume that under ordinary peacetime conditions the stock of plant and equipment in existence will always be large enough so that the capacity level of national product that we need to be concerned about will be fixed by the

---

[1] *Op. cit.,* Chapter III, Keynes presents the determination of the level of production as an aggregate supply and demand equilibrium adjustment. But the rest of the book emphasizes aggregate demand, particularly the consumption function and the marginal efficiency of capital. No aggregate supply schedule (or aggregate supply function) is presented after Chap. III.

productive capacity of the labor force. In general, businesses seem to plan their capital formation so as to be able to meet all the increases in demand that they anticipate. It will be convenient, too, despite frictional unemployment, to refer to a capacity level of aggregate demand as a full employment level.

I propose to try to show that business cycles and less-than-capacity operation are largely avoidable under our free enterprise system, that we can raise aggregate demand to approximately a full-employment level and can keep at or near that level. I propose to do this by suggesting a set of measures which, taken together, can bring about and maintain an adequate level of aggregate demand, a set of measures under which the profit system and market adjustments would continue to play the same dominant parts they play at present in determining the composition of our national product and in determining the way resources are used to produce our national product, and the distribution of income.

The principal measures in the program I shall offer for your consideration are all fiscal policy measures, federal government revenue and expenditure measures. Many economists would think a full employment program should rely to some extent also on monetary policy. Monetary policy has a place in the program I shall outline, but it is not a large one. Monetary policy, so far as it is pertinent here, consists of actions—chiefly actions by the Federal Reserve System—that tend either toward an easing or a tightening of credit. A tightening of credit restrains increases in aggregate demand. Theoretically, tight monetary policy could be used to bring about a decrease in aggregate demand but if it were, the result would almost certainly be a business recession. Practically, then, we should probably regard actions to tighten credit as confined to restraints on aggregate demand increases. Actions to ease credit do not by themselves constitute effective demand stimulants. Easy credit is a condition that is favorable to increases in aggregate demand. But a favorable condition alone is not a sufficient condition. A full employment program requires measures that will increase aggregate demand when it is inadequate, that will check increases if aggregate demand threatens to become too big, and perhaps that will decrease it if it should become too big. The easing and tightening of credit have a place in such a program, but it is a modest place.

The fiscal policy measures in the full employment program I shall offer for your consideration may be classified under three headings. First, there are measures that directly increase or decrease aggregate demand. These include changes in federal G.N.P. expenditures and in certain other product purchases. Second, there are increases and decreases in federal non-G.N.P. expenditures and decreases and increases in federal revenues, measures that add to or reduce the funds other sectors of the economy have to spend on G.N.P. purchases. And third, there are changes in federal taxes and subsidies that can alter the time-shape of the non-federal components of aggregate demand.

We can expect these various fiscal policy measures to require deficit financing at least part of the time. A countercyclical fiscal policy has sometimes been pictured as one involving deficits in Stages I, II, VIII, and IX of the cycle, and surpluses in Stages IV, V, and VI. One of the questions we must give attention to is whether we can expect to achieve full employment without an ever-mounting federal debt. We shall find that we cannot, on the basis of what is yet known about macro-economics, give a firm answer to this question. But we can be sure that the significance of debt increases has not infrequently been overstated. We can without qualification reject the argument that a fiscal policy that leads to an ever-mounting federal debt should be avoided because debt increases are dangerously inflationary. We can say with confidence that it is not federal debt increases that cause price increases. It is either demand-pull influences or cost-push influences. And so long as we have a less than full employment level of aggregate demand, any general increase in prices must be a result of cost-push influences. Government debt increases are irrelevant. There are, indeed, reasons for regarding an upward trend in federal debt as undesirable, particularly if it exceeds the trend in G.N.P. But so long as we have an inadequate level of aggregate demand, the dangers of inflation are not among them.

Moreover, as Lord Beveridge made clear, the balance of the central government's administrative budget is not the only budget balance we ought to be concerned about in deciding questions of fiscal policy.[2] We ought to be concerned also about avoiding a deficit in the national production budget, i.e., about avoiding a deficiency in aggregate demand. And quite possibly there may be need not only during a part of the business cycle but also as a continuing policy to choose between incurring a deficit in a fiscal sense and incurring a deficiency in aggregate demand.

A great variety of proposals have been advanced for achieving full employment. But it will be convenient for the present purpose to think of them as of two main types. There have been sufficient-stimulus proposals and there have been steering-wheel proposals. Both types rely on means of stimulating increases in aggregate demand. The difference between the two approaches to the objective of promoting full employment is that proponents of the sufficient-stimulus approach assume that the main problem is

[2] William H. Beveridge, *op. cit.*, especially paragraphs 181 to 190. The contrast here drawn is between the administrative budget of the central government and the economy's national production budget. For our present purpose it could be equally well drawn between the central government's cash budget and the national production budget.

merely one of increasing aggregate demand. Proponents of the steering-wheel approach assume there is also at times a problem of decreasing aggregate demand or, at any rate, of checking increases. Proponents of the steering-wheel approach rely on means of stimulating increases in G.N.P. some of the time, and on means of restraining increases in G.N.P. some of the time. In sufficient-stimulus proposals for achieving full employment, restraints have only minor roles, or no place at all. In his *General Theory* Lord Keynes proposed the sufficient-stimulus approach. He specifically opposed the use of tight-credit restraints on aggregate demand.[3]

Many economists besides Lord Keynes have been proponents of the sufficient-stimulus approach. But to my mind the steering-wheel approach is clearly preferable. It should be agreed that there may be only a small difference between a full-employment level of aggregate demand and one at which inflationary pressures are strong. It should be agreed, too, that while we know a great deal about the means that can be employed to stimulate increases in aggregate demand, we are far from knowing how strong a stimulus will be required to produce a given G.N.P. increase. Hence we must be able to follow a kind of trial and error approach. Suppose during one calendar quarter there is a deficiency in aggregate demand. Stimulants can be applied during the following quarter. If they should prove too strong, restraints can be applied in quarter no. 3. But, of course, the need in quarter no. 3 may be for stronger stimulants. Since we lack quantitative knowledge of the effects of stimulants and restraints we ought to be able to shift promptly from stimulation to restraint and vice versa, or to strengthen or weaken either the stimulants or the restraints as circumstances seem to indicate, i.e., we should adopt a steering-wheel approach.

[3] *Op. cit.,* Chapter 22, Section VI.

This statement takes the quarter as the national production budget adjustment period. If the adjustments are to iron out most of the business cycle, frequent adjustments—as often as once each quarter—are obviously needed. But there are administrative problems that increase with frequency. Monthly adjustments would, for many kinds of stimulants and restraints, be unduly difficult. In what follows I shall assume quarterly adjustments for most parts of the program I shall submit for your consideration.

Several of the parts in that program are designed primarily to moderate the cyclical fluctuations in G.N.P. But one of them is a way of making up a secular deficiency in aggregate demand, if, with the cycle largely ironed out, there should prove to be one. The four parts of the program I shall consider in this chapter are cycle-moderating measures.

Quite a number of economists seem to have assumed that business cycles are inevitable under our free enterprise form of organization. I see no reason to think so. I shall suggest a number of measures which taken together should be sufficient to eliminate most of the cycle. Three of them should serve substantially to reduce the cyclical fluctuations in those private components of aggregate demand that have been widest in past peacetime cycles, the demand for producers' and consumers' durable goods, the demand for new construction, and the increase in business inventories. Two of them are countercyclical proposals that would provide public components of aggregate demand that vary countercyclically.

One of the private demand proposals calls for procedures that would schedule most major private construction projects and most major durable goods purchases so as to avoid concentrating them in periods of high business activity. A federal agency—perhaps one established for the purpose—would have to be given responsibility for the scheduling procedures. This is not the only aggregate-demand scheduling responsibility I want to propose for it; I shall mention the others in a moment. Let us call it the G.N.P. Scheduling Agency. It would, of course, literally schedule only a fraction of the national output each quarter. But this agency should estimate all the components of G.N.P. it does not schedule and it should manage its scheduling of the components that are its direct concern in the light of these estimates.

There are two basic features of the scheduling responsibilities I propose for the G.N.P. Scheduling Agency. One is that the Agency would be clothed with the powers these responsibilities call for through voluntary agreements that would be entered into between the parties responsible for the components of aggregate demand involved on the one hand, and the G.N.P. Scheduling Agency on the other. The other is that the agency should employ business-like methods of publicity and salesmanship to persuade parties responsible for the types of demand involved to enter these agreements.[4] I propose three different types of agreement, one that has to do with major durable goods purchases and major private construction projects, one that has to do with business inventories, and one that is designed to provide for a shelf of works projects.

Agreements of the first type entered into during one calendar quarter would cover purchases to be made and construction work to be started during the following quarter. It will be convenient to refer to them as Definite Period Agreements. In a purchase agreement the purchaser would undertake to make his purchase before the end of the quarter, and the government would undertake, if he makes the purchase on scheduled time, to award him a small bonus or to grant him a small tax credit. The bonus or

---

[4] I made a proposal along these lines some years ago. See my article, "Business Stabilization by Agreement," *American Economic Review,* June, 1944, pp. 328–39.

tax credit might be 2 or 3 percent of cost. In the case of a construction agreement, the party responsible for the project would undertake not only to start work during the quarter following the signing of his agreement, but also to carry the work on and to complete it according to an appropriate schedule. If the project is one that will take a year or more to complete, there should be provision for making the bonus or tax credit available in installments. There should also be provision for amending the cost estimate and the schedule.

Let us consider for a moment the nature of the scheduling problem the G.N.P. Scheduling Agency would face under these Definite Period Agreements. Before entering into the capital formation agreements covering a quarter it should establish quotas, perhaps one quota for the durable goods purchases to be covered and one for construction projects. But possibly the quotas should be on a more detailed basis. Each quota should be that amount of capital formation which the Scheduling Agency estimates would take place, if the economy were to grow at the average rate that has prevailed during the past eight or ten years, but at an even rate without any cyclical fluctuations. In the case of construction work the quota should include work on projects already under way. The Scheduling Agency should seek to fill the quota for each type of capital formation it schedules, and should then stop scheduling. The bonuses or tax credits should apply only to scheduled durable goods purchases and scheduled construction projects. Indeed unscheduled purchases and projects of the types covered by the G.N.P. scheduling might well be subject to a small tax, say 3 percent *ad valorem*.[5] Of course, any private party that desired to avoid this tax could do so by deferring his purchase or the start of his project until the following quarter.

[5] In my original 1944 proposal this tax applied only to purchases and construction work that exceeded the quotas by more than 15 per cent.

The private party to each Definite Period Agreement would enter into it voluntarily, just as consumers voluntarily enter into purchase contracts with vendors. But vendors employ advertising and other forms of sales effort to make sales. I propose that the G.N.P. Scheduling Agency should do so. It should have a well-qualified sales force headed by a top-flight business executive. And it should be the concern of this staff to see that the terms of Definite Period Agreements are such as to make them attractive to prospective subscribers. I shall not attempt to suggest possible terms, except to note that in some types of agreements provision for government credit extension might be included. Even if nothing were done to reduce the cyclical fluctuations of other components of aggregate demand, this scheduling proposal should be able to effect a considerable reduction in the amplitude of fluctuation of the components it covers. And its effectiveness would be increased if something of consequence were done about the rest of aggregate demand.

This scheduling proposal has been confined to large projects and large purchases because it would be unduly expensive and cumbersome if it were made more comprehensive. For smaller durable goods purchases and smaller construction projects—I shall not attempt to say just how the lines between the large and the small should be drawn—a simpler procedure seems advisable. Credit would presumably continue to be tightened to discourage these types of final demand when discouragement is called for, and continue to be made easier to encourage them when encouragement is in order. But I suggest that countercyclical credit policy be supplemented by a countercycle in taxation. More specifically it is proposed that a tax be levied on purchases of small durable goods made and on work done on small construction projects during periods of high business activity and that a tax credit be granted for purchases of durables made and for construction work done during periods when business is particularly slack.

A flexible fiscal policy of this sort would not be feasible under present procedures for levying taxes. It is intended that the tax should discourage construction work and purchases of durables during one part of each business cycle and encourage these components of G.N.P. during another part of the cycle. Obviously it would not be possible for the Congress to pass a separate tax law to provide for each of the changes in taxation that this proposal calls for. The simplest way to provide the proposed fiscal flexibility involves giving some executive agency a certain amount of discretion over the taxation changes. The Congress might enact a revenue law that did these four things: 1) levied a tax on specific purchases made and specified construction work done during periods of high business activity; 2) granted a tax credit on such purchases made and construction work done during periods of particularly low business activity; 3) defined the periods of high activity and the periods of particularly low activity in broad, general terms; and 4) authorized and directed some executive agency to determine when a period of high activity existed, and when a period of particularly low activity existed. Under a revenue act of this nature the tax would be put into effect by a proclamation of an appropriate finding of fact, subject to a suitable notice. And it would be taken off by proclamation of another suitable finding of fact. Similarly with the tax credit. Presumably part of the time the tax would be in effect and part of the time the tax credit; but there would be periods in between to which neither the tax nor the tax credit applied.

Under a plan of this sort a small tax and a small tax credit would probably give sufficient incentives to reduce considerably the cyclical fluctuations in the kinds of capital formation covered, possibly 2 percent of cost for both tax and credit. We may note that a proclamation, during a cyclical upswing, that the tax would shortly go into effect might well cause bankers and other lenders to be more cautious, and so help to bring about some tightening of credit.

The principal problem of a plan such as this would appear to be political. The Congress would have to be persuaded to give some executive agency the requisite discretion over the timing of the tax and the tax credit. Since the Congress has been extremely loath to do anything that amounts to a delegation of any part of its taxing power, an alternative procedure for achieving fiscal flexibility has been proposed, a formula flexibility plan. Under this plan the Congress would define the conditions of high business activity and particularly low business activity very precisely. To illustrate, a period of particularly low business activity might be defined as one in which the unemployment rate exceeded 5 percent for three successive months. Under the formula flexibility plan the discretion vested in the executive agency would be reduced to the finding of very specific facts, such as this one. It should probably be added that there are other ways beside the formula plan in which the Congress might limit the grant of discretion. Thus there might be a 60-day period during which either house could act to prevent the application of the formula.

However, these political considerations are not really our present concern. Our immediate object is to outline a group of measures that together could be expected largely to iron out the business cycle. I have not undertaken to make a case for adopting such measures. The proposal to vary according to the business situation the tax incentives that bear on minor durable goods purchases and minor construction projects—to discourage these components of aggregate demand when business is brisk and encourage them when business is slack—should surely be included in our list of cycle-moderating measures.

Both this fiscal flexibility proposal and the Definite Period Agreement scheduling proposal have to do with fixed capital formation. But a major factor in the business fluctuations we have had since World War II has been the increases—plus and minus increases—in business inventories. My proposal here is for a second set of agreements, agreements between the businesses that hold the inventories, on the one hand and the G.N.P. Scheduling Agency, on the other. Let us call these Stable Inventory Agreements.[6] These agreements could cover only a limited range of inventories. Goods subject to rapid physical deterioration, e.g., green groceries, and goods subject to substantial depreciation through obsolescence could not be included in the plan. Staple materials and some foodstuffs, e.g., butter and margarine, presumably could be. Each subscriber to a Stable Inventory Agreement would undertake to keep the inventories covered by it intact during the term of the agreement. The G.N.P. Scheduling Agency would agree to pay the subscriber for so doing. It will be convenient to take as an illustration an agreement the subscriber to which maintains current physical quantity inventory records, and in which the amount of each inventory that is to be kept intact is specified in physical quantity terms. But there is no reason to assume that the plan would be restricted to agreements that could conveniently be worded in this way. Keeping the physical inventory of an item intact would mean having on hand at the end of each month a quantity equal to or greater than the quantity the subscriber had on hand at the same date a year earlier. But replacement of an item with a reasonable substitute should be permitted.

Let us consider the agreement provisions first from the government's viewpoint. Stable Inventory Agreements should cover as

[6] This proposal differs somewhat from the one I made in my 1944 article. Consequently, I have given the agreements a different name.

large a proportion of business inventories as possible. With suitable compensation and the year-ago rule it should be feasible to cover a very substantial part of the inventories of those goods that do not deteriorate rapidly and that are unlikely to become obsolete. After the plan gets under way a standard term for all Stable Inventory Agreements would probably be advisable. This should presumably be greater than the length of the average business cycle, i.e. greater than four years. I suggest a term of five years. But for the initial set of agreements I suggest various terms so that they would not all expire simultaneously. The other provisions of Stable Inventory Agreements of interest from the government's viewpoint are primarily administrative; provisions that would enable the G.N.P. Scheduling Agency to check on an inventory to determine whether it has actually been kept intact and provisions that would provide moderate penalties for violations.

From the subscriber's viewpoint the principal provisions in a Stable Inventory Agreement will clearly be those that fix what he gets paid for keeping his inventories intact. The total compensation paid during the term of an agreement should be sufficient to more than cover the cost of maintaining inventories during those months in which, in the absence of an agreement, the subscriber might want to reduce them below agreement levels. The compensation should cover interest on the inventory investment and inventory depreciation and insurance and property taxes during such months and should give the subscriber a small profit. It could be argued that the compensation should also cover a storage charge, but storage in this connection would seem to be a kind of overhead cost that would have to be met by the subscriber even if he were to liquidate his inventories. Presumably, in any case, if the agreement is one that specifies inventory maintenance levels in physical units, the compensation for each inventory item might well be stated as so much per unit per month. It would be difficult to make monthly payments only for those months during which the agreement is needed to prevent inventory liquidation. I suggest instead that the G.N.P. Scheduling Agency make a payment of so much per month every month during the term of the agreement. On the rough and arbitrary assumption that in the past periods of inventory liquidation and periods of inventory accumulation have been of nearly equal length, the amount of this payment might be fixed at half the estimated monthly carrying cost computation per unit of inventory for those months in which the subscriber might want to reduce it if there were no agreement. I think payments so determined would probably make Stable Inventory Agreements sufficiently attractive propositions. But, in any case, for each type of inventory the G.N.P. Scheduling Agency finds it both feasible to include in the plan and of sufficient importance to include, the agency should be given discretion to fix a sufficient monthly compensation rate to enable it to sell Stable Inventory Agreements. Possibly during the first year or so there should be promotional rates to get the inventory stabilization plan started.

It would probably be advisable for the Scheduling Agency to adopt standard formulas for fixing monthly compensation rates. For example, it might establish a number of broad classes of inventories, and for each class fix compensation rates as a definite percentage of unit value at the time the agreement is made. Even so, fixing monthly compensation rates for all inventory items of sufficient consequence to include in the plan would undoubtedly be a considerable undertaking for the G.N.P. Scheduling Agency. Undoubtedly, too, this is the kind of task that the agency could do better as it gained experience. It might be wise for a time to confine the plan to a limited number of items. It might be restricted at first to a select list of commodities that have shown wide fluctuations in the past: to major building materials and to a few non-building-material metal products, e.g., steel sheets and merchant bars.

From the subscriber's viewpoint the time at which a Stable Inventory Agreement is entered into will make a good deal of difference. An agreement would presumably be an unattractive proposition during a business recession. The plan might well be initiated in the early months of a cyclical upswing.

Two non-price terms that could be included in Stable Inventory Agreements and that would help to make them attractive may be suggested. One relates to credit. Inventories are liquidated during business recessions in part because the inventory holder needs the funds. The government might lend money to subscribers to Stable Inventory Agreements during recession periods to help them maintain their inventories. The inventories could be pledged as collateral for the loans. Possibly no interest should be charged.

The other suggestion relates to special situations in which maintaining inventories would involve hardship. For example, in the event of a strike the holder of an inventory agreement may need to use it and may temporarily be unable to make replacements. Each Stable Inventory Agreement should include a provision that would permit temporary depletion in such a situation, subject to the condition that while an inventory is below the agreement level, the monthly compensation payment on it would be discontinued, and to the further condition that replacement would be made somewhat promptly when circumstances permit.

One point that has been implied with regard to this Stable Inventory Agreement proposal should be made explicit. It is assumed that the sales staff of the G.N.P. Scheduling Agency would not only have the responsibility of fixing the compensation rates and of selling the agreements, but that it would also have a major part in designing the agreements. There should be a careful market analysis to determine what inventory items should be covered and when and how sales campaigns should be conducted; also to help in drawing the agreements in a way that would make them most attractive to prospective subscribers. But whatever is done by way of legitimate sales effort, each Stable Inventory Agreement would be a contract that has been entered into voluntarily by the subscriber.

So much for the three proposals aimed at substantially reducing the cyclical fluctuations in consumer durable goods purchases and private capital formation. They would have their immediate impacts on a large part of these components of aggregate demand that in the past have been particularly prominent contributors to the amplitudes of peacetime cycles—on a large part, but their coverage would not be complete. Some cyclical variations in private construction work and durable goods purchases and in the size of the inventory increment would still remain, also some cyclical variations in the rest of aggregate demand. I shall offer three other proposals for your consideration that would provide for varying countercyclically the components of aggregate demand they directly affect. These countercyclical variations should pretty fully offset whatever is left in the way of cyclical fluctuations. The six proposals together should very largely iron out the business cycle.

The countercyclical proposal I want to discuss now is for a works projects shelf.

Many discussions of the shelf idea assume that the projects that could be shelved are primarily public construction projects. Some people have claimed that we already have a shelf. They point to the needs for more schools and more and better roads and to the large volume of slum clearance and urban renewal work that ought to be undertaken. If one accepts the sufficient-stimulus view of the problem of inadequate demand, perhaps these potential projects can be called a shelf. But the shelf proposal is properly a countercyclical proposal, and certainly they do not provide a countercycle. That would mean getting them ready to go and then putting them on the shelf for awhile and taking them off according to a countercyclical schedule. If we are to have a shelf, we must have a way of putting projects onto it, and a way of taking them off. At present we have neither.

Many economists who have discussed the proposal for a public works countercycle have felt that it is not very practical. A considerable time may elapse before a public construction project can be ready to go. Getting legislative authorization and getting the plans drawn up and approved, the funds appropriated, and the contracts let may take well over a year. Also real estate may have had to be acquired, or perhaps there may have been need for a referendum. A business recession might be over before a project for which the preparatory steps took so long could get started. Moreover, once all these necessary, time-consuming preliminary steps have been taken the pressure is strong to get the project immediately under way. For many public works projects there are formidable difficulties in controlling their timing as a works projects countercycle would require.

My proposal for a works projects shelf is primarily a proposal for the control of project timing. It would provide a means of putting projects on the shelf and a means of taking them off. It does not apply to federal government projects. For state and local governments it includes such public construction projects as can meet its requirements. It also includes a variety of other undertakings. It is not a made-work proposal, but I think the experience with the WPA demonstrates that there are many public non-construction projects that could be included in a works projects shelf. Moreover, I see no reason for confining a shelf to public projects. My proposal includes private undertakings.

What I propose is still another form of agreement, an agreement between the project sponsor, on the one hand, a state or local government agency or a private party, and the G.N.P. Scheduling Agency, on the other hand. Let us call these Shelf Project Agreements.[7] From the government's viewpoint the principal provisions of Shelf Project Agreements are those that would give the Scheduling Agency control of project timing. Three such provisions are proposed: 1) The sponsor must show that the project is substantially ready to go, that so far as possible all necessary preliminary steps have been taken; 2) the sponsor must agree to defer the activation of the project until he receives a notice to activate it, provided that the deferment is not to exceed a specified maximum length of time; 3) the sponsor must agree to activate his project promptly on receipt of notice of its activation.

The principal provisions of a Shelf Project Agreement from the point of view of the sponsors are: 1) those that specify the compensation he will receive for deferring the activation of his project until he receives notice of activation and for prompt activation when he receives it; 2) the provision that specifies the maximum deferment period; and 3) the provisions that relate to the order in which projects are to be activated. Maximum periods of two, three, and possibly four years are suggested, the amount of the compensation increasing with the length of the period. On the average the compensation might be 10 percent of cost. In the case of a project that is likely to take as much as six months to complete there should probably be provision for progress payments. So far as order of project activation is concerned the main interest of subscribers is that it shall be fair. The G.N.P. Scheduling Agency may wish to establish several broad classes of two-year projects, and also of three- and four-year projects.

[7] In my 1944 article these were called Slack Period Reserve Agreements. The shorter and more easily understood title seems preferable.

Within each class the order of activation rule should be: first in, first out.

Some proposals for a projects shelf have assumed that the agency responsible for administering it would be expected to accept only projects that it finds of substantial merit. There would seem to be no reason for giving the G.N.P. Scheduling Agency any such responsibility. If the project sponsor is a state or local agency, it will have to get both legislative authorization for the project and appropriation of the necessary funds. If the sponsor is a private business enterprise, the enterprise will only undertake the project if it seems to promise a sufficient return to make the project worth-while. And if the sponsor is a non-profit organization—a university, for example—it will only sponsor a project that serves an objective to which the organization is committed.

The G.N.P. Scheduling Agency should not be asked to pass on the merits of proposed shelf projects. It should, however, set a minimum size limit. For administrative reasons it would clearly be unwise to include in the shelf a very large number of inconsequential projects.

Let us assume that the G.N.P. Scheduling Agency has the responsibility of selling Shelf Project Agreements and let us consider the scheduling problem it would have to deal with. In advance of each quarter it should estimate the prospects for the quarter. For the larger private construction projects and durable goods purchases there would be commitments under Definite Period Agreements. Also in appraising the business outlook, in addition to existing government expenditure programs and the existing tax structure, there would be the influence of Stable Inventory Agreements and the tax or tax credit on minor durables and construction work that would need to be taken into account. Possibly also there would be the influence of the countercyclical programs we shall be considering in the next chapter. At all events, the G.N.P. Scheduling Agency must estimate what the G.N.P. will be during the coming quarter. Let us suppose the estimate is made on the basis of existing commitments under Shelf Project Agreements and on the assumption of no new project activations. Let us suppose, too, that the Scheduling Agency estimates what the G.N.P. would be if there were no business cycle and if the economy's growth were to continue at the average rate that has prevailed in the past several years. To eliminate the cycle the volume of project activations should be sufficient to make up the difference between these two estimates.

In general there will be project activations every quarter. The volume will be increased if the estimate for the other components of G.N.P. is lower than for the previous quarter, and will be cut if the estimate for the other components is larger. The shelf could well include projects that take more than a year to complete, provided such projects do not constitute too large a part of the shelf. Probably the conditions for including a public construction project should be that the plans for it have been adopted and the funds for the first year of its operation have been appropriated. It should be noted that the appropriation of funds for a shelf project ought to take a special form. The appropriation act would have to specify that the funds would be available, not during the fiscal year to which most appropriations apply, but during the year (or some other period) following the activation of the project.

There will be projects activated each quarter. There should also be projects newly added to the shelf each quarter. The shelf will permit the volume of activations to exceed the volume of additions, but only for a limited time. With two- and three-year agreements the average turnover period for the shelf would probably be between two and three years, i.e., the average volume of activations per year would be less than half the average volume on the shelf. A sharp increase in activations not matched by an increase in additions could fairly quickly exhaust the shelf. If an average value of $30 billion of projects were to be added to the shelf each year it would be necessary to make substantially larger additions during the latter part of even a minor recession. Quite possibly it would be advisable to have two schedules of compensation rates, one that would apply most of the time, and one when there is need to increase the volume of new shelf projects.

It is to be assumed that from time to time the G.N.P. Scheduling Agency would make a careful market analysis to determine what kinds of projects could be included in the shelf, and what the terms of Shelf Project Agreements should be to make them attractive to potential subscribers. One obvious possibility here, too, is that the government might extend credit to help in financing the projects. Also the Scheduling Agency might make information available about any project conducted successfully in one place that might well be repeated elsewhere. I have suggested an average figure of $30 billion per year of new projects. Let me mention some illustrative types. For a state government, there might be a park development, a deer population census, a stream pollution clean-up and reforestation; for a city, a real property inventory, slum clearance, and a mosquito eradication campaign. For universities there are a variety of research project possibilities, also various extensive statistical tabulation jobs. The principal possibilities for large businesses would doubtless be construction projects, but it should be possible to devise a form of Shelf Project Agreement that would provide for scheduling a firm's maintenance work so that much of it would come at the bottom of the cycle instead of at the top as it has commonly done in the past. Surely there is a sufficient variety of potential shelf projects to make a $30 billion shelf entirely feasible; perhaps, if that should be needed to iron out the cycle, a very much larger shelf.

I have not proposed including federal projects in the shelf, because there seems to be no way to give the G.N.P. Scheduling Agency control over their timing without giving it what amounts to a kind of appropriation power for financing them.[8] The most feasible plan would seem to be that the Congress should direct some federal agencies to time-specified expenditures so that they will reinforce the operations of the shelf. Thus the General Services Administration might well be directed, so far as consistent with its other responsibilities, so to time its construction expenditures. Also the Defense Department might be directed to vary the number of persons being given military training countercyclically. This second proposal assumes it would apply only in a peacetime situation. And it should be noted that, if the preparedness objective is to have a particular number of trainees available each year, it would be possible by increasing slightly the average annual number of persons inducted for training to meet this objective every year and at the same time make quite substantial year-to-year variations in the number of inductees.

Arranging to have federal expenditure programs synchronize approximately with the shelf operations would doubtless entail political difficulties. But the programs for which such arrangements could be worked out may fairly be considered a part of the shelf proposal. And the shelf, including these programs, together with the three proposals for reducing the cycle in the private components of aggregate demand, constitutes the program I am proposing specifically for ironing out cyclical fluctuations in United States business activity. In appraising the probable

[8] There were, of course, federal WPA projects, but the WPA had what amounted to a delegated appropriation power.

adequacy of the effect of their combined operation, one should have in mind that that effect would involve a kind of multiplier. The process of expansion of business activity during a cyclical upswing involves one; so does the process of cyclical contraction. Consequently, the reduction in the fluctuations in aggregate demand resulting from the three private demand proposals should be somewhat larger than that in private construction, durable goods purchases, and business inventory increases alone. Moreover, there should be a countercyclical multiplier effect as a consequence of the operation of shelf projects. The question whether the net result of the operation of shelf projects and the three private demand proposals could substantially eliminate the business cycle is evidently a quantitative one. Is it reasonable to suppose that the shelf could be large enough and the timing of its operation precise enough for an affirmative answer to this question? Is it reasonable to visualize a situation in which the only kinds of unemployment of consequence that would remain would be frictional unemployment and perhaps unemployment due to a continuing secular deficiency in aggregate demand? I think it definitely is. Surely the plan I have suggested for the shelf would provide for sufficiently precise control of the timing of projects, if not during the period immediately following its inauguration, at any rate, after the G.N.P. Scheduling Agency had gained experience with it.

But possibly you are thinking that the decrease in the cyclical fluctuations of the private components of aggregate demand that could be brought about by my three proposals for these components would be too small or else that the projects shelf would be too small fully to iron out the cycle. This is not, I think, very likely. But it is a possibility I shall deal with in the next chapter.

One of the two proposals I shall discuss in Chapter Three is countercyclical. But it is aimed primarily, not at the cycle in productive activity in this country, but at the cycle in our demand for other countries' products. It could help some on our domestic cycle, but not a great deal. It is a proposal for international action, rather than for action by the United States alone.

The other proposal I shall discuss in Chapter Three should, I think, be regarded as primarily a proposal for making up a secular deficiency in aggregate demand, if with the cycle largely eliminated there should prove to be such a deficiency. It is a proposal for adjusting aggregate demand to the right level by increasing or decreasing personal consumption expenditure. It would do this by increasing or decreasing disposable income. If there should be some of the business cycle remaining to be dealt with, this proposal could deal with it.

To the question, "Can we under our free enterprise type of economic organization adopt measures that will substantially eliminate the business cycle?," I answer "Yes."

Chapter Three

An Adequate Aggregate Employment Program

IN CHAPTER ONE we noted various steps that could be taken to reduce the minimum amount of frictional unemployment that would remain if aggregate demand were raised to and kept at a full capacity level. In Chapter Two we examined four measures that together should iron out a very large part of the cyclical fluctuations in United States business activity. Now I want to propose two other measures to round out the full employment program I am offering for your consideration. One of them is designed to deal with a part of the business-cycle problem that involves world markets for basic raw materials and foodstuffs, a part that seems to require international action. The other should be capable of smoothing out any cyclical fluctuations in United States business activity not entirely eliminated by this international action operating in conjunction with the four measures we have already considered. But it would also be capable of remedying any longer-term, secular deficiency in aggregate demand that might remain when the business cycle has been eliminated.

In this chapter I want also to comment briefly on the costs and gains of a full employment program of the type I am proposing.

There have been notoriously wide cyclical fluctuations in the prices of the basic raw materials and foodstuffs for which there are world markets and in the incomes of the people who produce these commodities. The international action I want to propose to reduce these fluctuations is a form of buffer stock operation. In connection with the four cycle-moderating measures we considered in the last chapter we noted that they would be mutually reinforcing. We may anticipate our consideration of the buffer stock proposal by noting that it would participate in this mutual reinforcement. To the extent that cyclical fluctuations in our aggregate demand are reduced there would be a reduction in the fluctuations in the U.S. demand for basic raw materials and foodstuffs. And to the extent that cyclical fluctuations in the incomes of U.S. producers would be reduced by the buffer stock proposal there would be a reduction in the cyclical fluctuations of the personal consumption expenditures of these producers. But as I have already suggested this would be a relatively small contribution to the ironing out of our domestic business cycle.

The form of buffer stock operation I propose is part of a plan for a combined stock-piling arrangement and a world currency advanced by Benjamin Graham more than twenty years ago.[1] The stock-piling part of his plan is quite separable from the world currency part, and taken separately, is a buffer stock operation that has significant advantages over possible alternatives. No doubt there is much to be said for some form of world currency. But I see serious difficulties in the form Graham has proposed. Going into them, however, would entail a considerable digression. Let me simply say that the currency part of Graham's plan impresses me as one of the many proposals for monetary reform based on the apparently intriguing assumption that changing our monetary system is the way to eliminate business cycles. I have already made clear that I do not think any monetary reform alone could do much about cyclical fluctuations in aggregate demand.

A buffer stock operation for any commodity involves an agency that will be on the demand side of the market for it and will stock-pile it when the market is weak and, when the market is strong, will be on the supply side and will reduce its stock pile. In the kind of operation I have in mind the agency would establish two prices to govern its buying and selling, a support price and a higher ceiling price. The agency would announce its readiness to buy as much during any weak-market period as the market would supply at its predetermined support price; likewise its readiness to sell during any strong-market period, so long as its stock pile lasts, whatever the market would take at its predetermined ceiling price. If the agency is adequately financed the market price for the commodity will never go below the agency's support price. And when demand is brisk, the market price will not rise above the agency's ceiling price, unless and until its

[1] Benjamin Graham, *World Commodities and World Currency* (New York, 1944).

stock pile is completely liquidated. If the buffer stock operation
has been established during a period of slack demand, and if the
support price and the ceiling price are both high enough, the
market price will be pegged between these two limiting figures.
For the moment it may suffice to say that the mistake of setting
the support and ceiling prices too low in a buffer stock operation
has not been the usual one. The tendency has been to set them
too high.

All four of the cycle-moderating proposals we have so far
considered were proposed for adoption by the United States act-
ing alone. None of them, in the present unorganized state of
world affairs, could easily be operated on an international scale.
But a buffer stock operation would involve only international
action of a sort for which there is ample precedent. And since
the markets for the commodities to be dealt with are world
markets, an international buffer stock agency seems needed. Let
us call this agency the International Commodity Stabilization
Corporation. It could be organized much as the International
Monetary Fund and the International Bank for Reconstruction
and Development have been organized. Countries that wished to
participate in the buffer stock operation would become member
countries. They would subscribe to its capital stock and arrange
for the selection of its governing board. The principal organiza-
tional problem would be that of providing sufficient capital. In
1944 Graham mentioned an inventory figure of $5 to $7 billion
for his plan. Assuming that the Stabilization Corporation would
operate, as he proposed, in some 15 to 25 basic commodities,
and allowing for the growth of world trade, for price increases,
and for contingencies Graham did not foresee, let us say that the
initial capital fund should be approximately $30 billion.

The list of 15 commodities Graham thought should probably
be covered to begin with included: wheat, corn, cotton, wool,

rubber, sugar, coffee, tea, tin, and wood pulp.[2] He based his suggestions on relative importance in world trade and world production. Certainly this should be a primary consideration. But I think another, and perhaps equally important, consideration should be the need for any further price stabilizing influence in the case of a commodity in the existing market for which there are already arrangements that do a good deal to stabilize its price. It would seem reasonable that the list of commodities covered by the Stabilization Corporation's operations should not include commodities whose prices are clearly administered prices.

There is another commodity coverage consideration that should doubtless apply, although not to the operations of the Stabilization Corporation, but to those of the U.S. G.N.P. Scheduling Agency in connection with its Inventory Stabilization Agreements. There would probably not be much reason to have the same commodity covered by both, and on a jurisdictional question of this sort the U.S. Scheduling Agency should presumably defer to the International Stabilization Corporation.

But I have not yet stated the distinctive feature of the Graham buffer stock proposal. It would not attempt to peg the price of any single commodity covered by the plan between a lower and upper figure. Instead it would peg what amounts to a price index. The Stabilization Corporation would not engage in buying and selling individual commodities; it would buy and sell packages, each package consisting of specified quantities of the various covered commodities. Graham calls the packages bales. Before it begins to operate, the Stabilization Corporation would establish the precise composition of a bale. It would doubtless use the metric system in doing this, but for our present purpose it is con-

---

[2] Graham's leading commodity list included also tobacco, petroleum, coal, pig iron, and copper. In addition to this leading commodity list he offered a list of not quite so important commodities.

venient to speak in terms of the foot-pound-second system. A bale would consist of a specified number of pounds of coffee, a specified number of bushels of wheat, a specified number of long tons of crude (natural) rubber, etc. The Stabilization Corporation would deal only in whole bales. It would announce a bale support price and a bale ceiling price. During any month it would buy as many bales at its support price as sellers would sell to it, and after it had acquired a stock pile it would sell as many bales as buyers would take at its ceiling price, so long as the stock pile lasted. The support price and the ceiling price would be set on the basis of careful analyses of the market situations and market prospects for the various covered commodities. If these two prices are set with sufficient wisdom and foresight the price of the bale would be pegged between these limiting figures.

Something needs to be said about the problem of setting the bale support and ceiling prices. But first there are a number of complications that ought to be pointed out and commented on. What is a bushel of wheat or a pound of coffee? Where would it be stored? And under what arrangements? In what currency should the support and ceiling prices be stated? Presumably the Stabilization Corporation would want to prescribe the specifications to which each covered commodity would have to conform. Presumably, too, it would want to exercise a considerable measure of control over storage places and storage arrangements. As for the currency, since the proposal I am outlining does not include the monetary part of Graham's plan, the two prices should undoubtedly be stated in U.S. dollars.

It is a well-established principle of index number making that a relatively short list of time series may suffice for the construction of an acceptable price index, but that a very long list may be required for the construction of an acceptable physical volume index. Something like this principle is pertinent here. The mar-

ket price of a commodity bale would be, in effect, a Laspeyres
price index of the covered commodities, the physical quantities
that define the composition of the bale for purposes of computing
its price being the weights. We can reasonably assume that wheat
would be one of the commodities. Four specified physical quantities—i.e. four time series—should suffice for wheat, one at
Kansas City, one at Buenos Aires, one at Winnipeg, and one at
Sydney. Other commodities would be handled similarly—one
specified quantity in the principal market in each major producing country. To determine the market price of a commodity
bale at any date the market prices of the individual commodities in pounds, pesos, etc., would, of course, have to be translated
into U.S. dollars at current exchange rates. When the bale's price
so computed declined to the support-price level the Stabilization
Corporation would make bale purchases; when the bale's price
rose to the ceiling-price level the Corporation would sell.

But as you have doubtless noticed, I have skipped over one
point about the way the composition of a commodity bale for
purposes of computing its price would have to be stated. The
physical quantity of any commodity in any central market should
be stated as so and so many units of a particular specification
of the commodity. Thus the quantity of wheat in Kansas City
would probably be stated as so many bushels of No. 2 hard and
dark winter wheat. In effect, the Kansas City price quotation for
No. 2 hard winter wheat would be taken to represent U.S. wheat
prices.

The list of central market commodity specifications included
for purposes of computing the price of a bale could, I think, be
a fairly short one; 50 or 60 specifications might well suffice. But
note that the bale is defined in one way for these purposes, in
another for actual purchases and sales. There would be many
varieties of actual commodites stored, and they would be stored

in a great many different places. The Stabilization Corporation would want to prescribe the several varieties of each commodity it would be prepared to accept, and the minimum acceptable quality standards. And it would want to prescribe the locations in which it would allow storage and the standards the storage facilities would have to meet. We may assume that from the time the Corporation acquires title to a particular commodity bale until the time it is sold, the Corporation would assume responsibility for the costs connected with its storage. Presumably the Corporation would be concerned, among other things, in prescribing standards for storage facilities, to regulate storage costs.

No doubt you have been wondering who would sell whole bales to the Commodity Stabilization Corporation when the markets for the commodities in the bales were weak, and who would buy whole bales when these markets were strong. Graham's answer is that with the establishment of this kind of buffer stock operation, commodity brokers would find it profitable to package the individual commodities into bales when the commodity markets were weak, and to acquire the bales and sell their constituents when the markets were strong. This seems a convincing answer, but we should recognize what it implies. The Stabilization Corporation's purchases and sales would peg the price of a bale, not between its support price and its ceiling price, but between appreciably wider limits. There would have to be a selling margin and a purchase margin for the brokers.

I have suggested that, in buffer stock operations for individual commodities, there has been a tendency to set support prices too high and also, in effect at least, to set ceiling prices too high. But probably it should be said that the operations I have in mind are, properly speaking, not buffer stock operations. The objective has frequently been, not to stabilize the price of the commodity, but to raise it, for the operation has commonly been organized or at any rate pressed for by the producers of the commodity. This can be said of schemes that involve no stock piling, of course. But they should not be counted in the present connection. When a plan involves stock piling and has a support price and a ceiling price that are too high, the result is bound to be stock accumulation with little or no stock liquidation. A major problem in a buffer stock operation, assuming a low enough ceiling price to call for inventory liquidation when the market is strong, is that of adhering to the ceiling price and carrying out the liquidation it calls for.

There are three main advantages in Graham's commodity bale proposal. One relates to pressures. In general, pressures from the producer side of a market are far stronger than those from the consumer side. The bale proposal does not equalize the pressures, but it somewhat diminishes the difference, both in connection with setting the prices and when it is a question of adhering to a ceiling price. The producer pressures are more diffuse because what is at stake is a price index, not a particular commodity price.

The second advantage of the bale proposal has to do with the wisdom with which the support and ceiling prices are set, assuming they are set as well as available facts permit. If separate support and ceiling prices were to be set for each of the 50 or 60 central market commodity specifications, it can reasonably be expected that some of them would be too high, others too low. To the extent that the errors would be offsetting, the bale prices would be better than the determinations for the individual commodity specifications by virtue of these offsets.

The third advantage of the bale proposal is that while the bale price would be pegged between a figure a little below the bale support price and a figure a little above the bale ceiling price, the price of each individual variety of each covered commodity would be free, within wide limits, to vary in response to changes in the special conditions affecting the supply of and the demand for it. It is true that the synchronous cyclical fluctuations in the prices of the varieties of the covered commodities in response to the common stimulus of changes in aggregate world demand would be substantially reduced. But the prices would continue to reflect supply and demand changes that affect the relations of each commodity specification to other commodity specifications. And this, many of us would say, is as it should be.

The amount by which the bale ceiling price exceeded the bale support price would determine the operating revenue of the Stabilization Corporation. Graham suggested a spread of approximately 10 percent.[3] If the Corporation's inventory had an average turnover period of two years, a 10 percent spread would provide a revenue equal to 5 percent of the investment, quite possibly not enough to cover storage and other operating costs. If not, the deficiency would have to be made up by an assessment —presumably a small one—on the members of the Corporation. The alternative would be a slightly wider spread. Whether this alternative would be preferable as a matter of public policy is a question we do not need to go into, since we are not trying to settle policy questions. A wider spread would mean a slight reduction in the price stabilizing effectiveness of the buffer stock operation.

The precise composition of the commodity bale and its support price would have to be decided before the Stabilization Corporation started to operate. Presumably the ceiling price should be agreed upon at that time, too. But after a number of years, in view of changing supply and demand conditions, new

---

[3] Specifically Graham proposed the establishment of a parity price with the ceiling price 5 per cent above it and the support price 5 per cent below.

prices and a new bale composition might be advisable. I will not attempt to consider the problems these changes would involve, except to say that the changes should not be very frequent. I suggest that the initially-established prices should be adhered to for at least three years, and that the initially-established bale composition should be kept for a rather longer period, let us say five years.

So much for the price stabilizating activities of the International Commodity Stabilization Corporation that I propose as part of my full employment program. Let us suppose for the moment that this and the four parts we considered in Chapter Two have been adopted and have for some time been in operation. Would there be any cycle left in U.S. business activity? And would there be a secular deficiency in the level of aggregate demand? Quite possibly the cycle would not, under these circumstances, be entirely ironed out. But it is reasonable to conclude that the cyclical fluctuations that remained would be extremely mild. At recent cyclical peaks there has been a substantial amount of unemployment, a good deal that could not be called merely frictional. In May, 1960, 5.1 percent of our civilian labor force was unemployed. I venture the guess that fully two-fifths of the unemployment at this cyclical peak date was due to the deficiency in aggregate demand. It is not entirely safe to infer from peak date figures that there would be such a deficiency if most of the cycle were eliminated. But as things stand today a deficiency seems quite likely.

All five of the measures we have considered for reducing cyclical fluctuations in employment and business activity may be said to operate by changing the timing of particular components of aggregate demand. Except for the minor income effects of the bonuses offered by the G.N.P. Scheduling Agency, none of them averaged over the cycle would add to any particular component of G.N.P. To deal with a secular deficiency in aggregate demand such an addition is called for. Conceivably the addition could be made to any of the four main components of G.N.P., but there are strong reasons for holding that most of the increase should be an increase in personal consumption expenditure, and that it should be brought about by an increase in disposable personal income.

Toward the close of World War II a considerable number of proposals for achieving full employment were advanced. One of them, made by John Pierson, was a proposal for adjusting the level of G.N.P. upward (or downward) by increasing (or decreasing) disposable personal income.[4] Part VI of the full employment program I offer for your consideration is Pierson's proposal.

The reasons for holding that, when there is need for increasing aggregate demand to raise it to a capacity level, most of the increase should be in personal consumption expenditure, are partly negative. It should be generally agreed that it would be unwise to attempt to bring about even a part of the increase through autarchic measures to add to our export surplus. It should be generally agreed, also, that we could not expect most of the increase in G.N.P. to take the form of increased private capital formation. Our present concern is with a secular, not merely a temporary, increase in aggregate demand. Therefore we should regard substantially the whole of any capital formation increase as derived demand, i.e., as providing the means of producing the goods and services included in the other components of aggre-

---

[4] John H. G. Pierson, "The Underwriting of Consumer Spending as a Pillar of Full Employment Policy, *American Economic Review,* March, 1944, pp. 21–55. Attention is directed to the fact that Lord Beveridge's book, Benjamin Graham's book, and my article cited above, as well as Pierson's article, were all published in 1944.

gate demand. At all events it would be difficult to plan a secular increase in investment except as a means of providing additional productive capacity.

The reasons why it would be unwise to have any considerable secular increase in aggregate demand take the form of government G.N.P. expenditures are more complicated. They have to do with the difficulties of deciding what specific additional goods and services the government should buy. Presumably the government should not make expenditures on facilities that would compete with private enterprise and discourage private capital formation. So far as other government G.N.P. expenditures are concerned, I think they should not be increased just for the purpose of adding to aggregate demand. If there is first a decision that a particular additional dollar total is to be spent, and then subsequently a determination of the objects of expenditure, the choice of expenditure objects is unlikely to be very wise. The process of choosing the objects of expenditure is likely to be a kind of pork-barrel operation in which log-rolling plays an important part. And the result is likely to include a good many projects that are essentially boondoggles.

During the decade ending with 1964 private capital formation was approximately one-seventh of the total G.N.P. Let us assume that if an increase of x billion dollars per year in aggregate demand is needed to raise the national product to capacity level, something like one-seventh of that amount might take the form of private capital formation, and that the remainder would be either consumer expenditures or government expenditures, or else a combination of the two. For government expenditures there are the unsavory difficulties just noted. There are also positive reasons for preferring to have the increase in consumer expenditures. Let us assume that this is brought about by an addition to disposable income—we will shortly consider how such an addition might be brought about. No public policy decision regarding the composition of the expenditure program would be involved; the individual consumers would make the decisions. And while the proposition that the individual consumer can make wiser decisions to serve his own best interest than any government official could make for him needs substantial qualifications, it also contains a large element of truth. Let us grant, among other things, that there are goods that need to be purchased collectively and that there are purchases consumers should not be permitted to make. Let us grant some other qualifications, too. Subject to a few not very restrictive limitations it seems reasonable to assume that the individual consumer is the best judge of his own best interest. Subject to a few not very restrictive limitations we regard consumer's freedom of choice as a freedom that we especially prize. The case for having about six-sevenths of any needed secular increase in aggregate demand decided by consumers' free choice is a very appealing one.

There are two principal ways in which disposable personal income might be increased: a) through a tax cut, and b) through an income subsidy. Pierson considered particularly a cut in federal, personal taxes and what for simplicity I will call a per capita subsidy payment. He assumed that the size of the cut or subsidy payment would be adjusted for each quarter on the basis of the latest available information on the level of employment at the time of making the adjustment. One advantage of the subsidy alternative is that it would be easier from the administrative viewpoint to make the quarterly adjustments than in the case of the tax cut, unless the cut took some such form as that of a fixed amount per taxpayer. Another and perhaps more significant advantage to the subsidy is that it would reach even the lowest income bracket. It would reach, among others, those who had little or no employment income. It may be added that the subsidy would result in an appreciably larger increase in personal consumption expenditures per dollar of cost in terms of the federal budget. But for our present purpose we do not need to decide which of these alternatives is preferable, or whether there is some other form of subsidy or tax cut that would be better than either. It is clear that a quarterly per capita subsidy could be used to make whatever quarterly adjustments might be called for to increase disposable income. So could a tax cut. For our present purpose that is all we need to say about methods of increasing disposable income.

Let us take the per capita income subsidy by way of illustration, and consider how the G.N.P. might be adjusted quarter by quarter. We are supposing the other parts of the program I have proposed are in operation. It will be convenient to suppose, too, that discretion to determine the amount of the income subsidy is vested in the G.N.P. Scheduling Agency. Somewhat in advance of each quarter the agency's first step would be to determine the G.N.P. objective for the quarter. Next the agency would estimate all the components of aggregate demand for the quarter except the demand represented by shelf project operations. It would probably make this estimate on the assumption that the amount of the per capita income subsidy was to be the same as in the previous quarter. Then it would decide on the volume of shelf project activations, and would add the estimated resulting demand to that for the other components of G.N.P. To complete its planning for the coming quarter, the Scheduling Agency would determine what change in the per capita subsidy payment, if any, would be needed to make the estimate for total G.N.P. equal to the quarter's objective.

We have been supposing that the other parts of the full employment program I have outlined would iron out most, if not all, of the cycle in U.S. business activity, and that the subsidy would serve primarily to make up a secular deficiency in aggregate demand. If there were no cycle left the per capita subsidy fixed by the Scheduling Agency would change very little from quarter to quarter, but whatever cyclical fluctuation remained could be handled by countercyclical variations in the amount of the quarterly subsidy payment. Conceivably there would be no need for a constant quarterly payment.

Let us take account of the possibility of a situation in which there would be neither any cycle nor any secular deficiency in aggregate demand. If recent unemployment data make this seem an unlikely contingency, let me note two considerations that might tend to favor it. One is that ironing out the cycle could theoretically bring about a secular increase in the level of G.N.P. The question whether a prospective capital investment promises an adequate return depends on the expected capacity factor. Ironing out the cycle should improve investment prospects by improving this factor, i.e., by decreasing the amount of expected idle capacity time. Hence it should make projects pay that do not pay today.

The other consideration relates to what is commonly called Say's Law. Of course, it is not a law because it is not a valid generalization about the way a free enterprise economy behaves. It assumes aggregate demand is alway tending to equal aggregate productive capacity. We know this is not true in a cyclical sense, but there is probably something in the idea in a secular sense. As a long-run trend, aggregate demand—measured at constant prices—has had about the same growth rate as aggregate productive capacity.

I have suggested the possibility of a situation in which there might be no secular deficiency in aggregate demand. Let me go further. I think we should take account of the possibility of a level of aggregate demand that seriously taxes the economy's productive capacity. Pierson considered such a possibility and suggested what he called a spendings tax as a way to deal with it. In general the arguments for making up a deficiency in aggregate demand by increasing disposable income suggest decreasing disposable income as a way to eliminate a demand surplus. Its effectiveness for the purpose does not seem open to question. And we need not consider whether a spendings tax would be the best way to reduce disposable income from the viewpoint of public policy.

The full employment program that I offer for your consideration, then, consists of three kinds of Scheduling Agency agreements, one of them to provide implementation for a works projects shelf; a busy period tax and slack period tax credit; a buffer stock operation; and a consumer income subsidy. I think that together they would practically eliminate both the cycle and any secular deficiency in aggregate demand, and that they would provide for a sufficiently precise control of aggregate demand not only to keep it at a full capacity level, but also to prevent serious inflationary pressures.

Let me conclude what I have to say about the possibility of achieving full employment under our free enterprise system with some comments on the subject of costs and gains. I will consider this subject first in a federal budget, billions of dollars sense, and then in a more general, less definitely measurable sense.

My guesses about dollar costs and revenues—they relate mainly to costs—will be confined to the six adequate demand proposals. It is true that several of the tentative suggestions I have made for reducing the unavoidable minimum amount of frictional unemployment would involve federal government expenditures. But the dollar total would be relatively small, at least in comparison with the budget expenditures the adequate demand proposals would require.

It will be well to deal with the cycle and any remaining secular deficiency separately. In regard to the former, let us suppose that Definite Period Agreements might cover half of private construction and durable goods purchases. These totalled some $140 billion in 1964. A 2½ percent bonus on $70 billion would come to $3.5 billion. Let us suppose, too, that there might be around $50 billion of new shelf projects each year. If the average bonus rate were 10 percent, this would mean $5 billion in bonuses. Again, let us suppose some $50 billion of inventories covered by Stable Inventory Agreements and monthly compensation rates under these agreements averaging ⅓ percent per dollar of covered inventory. On these assumptions total annual compensation under Stable Inventory Agreements would be $2 billion. Obviously these cost guesses are very rough, and it is not worth while to attempt to be at all precise about the other three proposals. We might take the slack period tax credits for minor durable goods purchases and construction projects and the busy period taxes on these forms of demand to be about equal. And we might assume the International Commodity Stabilization Corporation to be not far from self-supporting. Just how the part of the personal income subsidy that could be attributed to ironing out the cycle ought to be counted is not at all clear. Let us put it at a fairly high figure to make some allowance for the administrative costs of the whole program, say one-third of the total of the three definite cost figures I have suggested, that is, one-third of $10.5 billion. And let us make no allowance for any U.S. assessment for support of the Stabilization Corporation. I propose, then, a comprehensive gross total figure of $14 billion, or about 2¼ percent of the 1964 G.N.P. It is gross because there would probably be some offsets, particularly increased taxes. But I think it should be recognized too that the gross dollar budget cost of smoothing out the business cycle might quite possibly turn out to be somewhat more than 2¼ percent of the G.N.P.

The reason why I have suggested a separate dollar figure for handling the cycle part of the full employment problem is that, whatever the cost, there should be no question about the possibility of covering it by increased taxes. It can be argued that imposing higher taxes to finance the various cycle-reducing measures would have the effect of increasing any secular deficiency in aggregate demand. But if the added taxes were reasonably well timed, they would certainly not make the problem of smoothing out the cycle more difficult. Indeed, they might well make some contribution to the elimination of cyclical fluctuations.

There is, of course, a technical problem in fiscal policy: how to balance the budget over the cycle by making the surpluses, while business is brisk, offset the slack-period deficits. On this point I shall merely repeat a proposal I made a long time ago—the budget expenditures that are large when business is poor, e.g., the Scheduling Agency's bonus payments, can be treated as deferred charges. Such expenditures during each year can then be written off during, say, the following ten years, and the write-offs of these expenditures can be accelerated when business is good.[5] There should be no significant cycle problem in connection with these write-offs. If the write-offs, and not the actual out-of-pocket outlays for bonuses, etc., are treated as budget expenditures, the problem of balancing the budget over the cycle should present no special difficulty. My conclusion, then, is that we can not only substantially iron out the business cycle, but also that we can do so, if that is considered wise public policy, on a balanced budget basis.

The budget cost of making up a secular deficiency in aggregate

[5] "The Capital Budget and the War Effort," *American Economic Review*, March, 1943, pp. 38–49.

demand, if there should turn out to be one with the cycle eliminated, would obviously depend on the size of the deficiency. Let
us assume the per capita subsidy method of increasing disposable
income is used. We can say that each billion dollars of deficiency
would require an income subsidy outlay of x dollars, where x
depends on two quantities: the marginal propensity to consume
and the derived demand ratio. Let us suppose a marginal propensity to consume of 90 percent and a derived demand ratio of
one-seventh. Then $\frac{6}{7}$ of the deficiency $= \frac{9}{10}$ of the subsidy outlay. Hence the subsidy outlay required would be equal to $\frac{60}{63}$
times the deficiency. A billion-dollar annual secular deficiency
in aggregate demand would require an annual subsidy outlay of
nearly a billion dollars. Since we do not know how big the
deficiency might be, we cannot say much more than this about
dollar cost.

Thus far very little has been done to explore the question
whether a billion-dollar outlay to make up a secular deficiency
in aggregate demand could be tax financed.[6] There is a good reason for thinking a per capita income subsidy of a billion dollars
financed by an individual income tax yield increase of a billion
dollars would result in some increase in personal consumption
expenditures, particularly if the entire tax yield increase was not
the result of an increase in the rate applicable to the lowest

[6] Lord Beveridge, in his *Full Employment in a Free Society,* assumed
that it could be. So did Nicholas Kaldor who wrote an appendix for him
on this point. Explorations of the question to date have been mainly in
the form of a priori model analyses. For an illustration of this way of
dealing with the problem see William Salant, "Taxes, Income Determination, and the Balanced Budget Theorem," *Review of Economics and
Statistics,* May, 1957. Reprinted in the American Economic Association's
Readings in Business Cycles, ed. by Lawrence R. Klein and Robert A.
Gordon (Homewood, Illinois, 1965).

bracket. The marginal propensity to consume apparently decreases slightly as per capita income increases. But we could not be at all sure today about the quantitative effect of an x billion dollar per capita income subsidy financed by a particular set of individual income tax bracket rate increases. And we could say still less about the G.N.P. increase that would result from a tax-financed per capita income subsidy of x billion dollars, if the added taxes were less direct. Should there be a public policy decision in favor of a full employment program somewhat along the lines of the one that I have proposed, an early order of business ought surely to be investigating the question whether a subsidy to make up a secular deficiency in aggregate demand could be tax financed without nullifying its effectiveness.

Our conclusions regarding a secular deficiency in aggregate demand, then, must be somewhat indefinite. We cannot say, if the cycle were eliminated, how big the remaining secular deficiency would be; cannot even be certain there would be one. And we cannot say whether there is an upper limit to the size of the secular deficiency that could be made up by a tax-financed income subsidy.

So much for the dollar costs and revenues of full employment that would show in the federal government budget. Lord Beveridge emphasized the need to consider also the economy's budget. What about that?

There is in the first place a major gain. A part of this can be estimated—in fact has been estimated—in quantitative terms. We can say what we think the addition to the G.N.P. would be if we succeeded in operating our economy continuously at a level that fully utilized the productive capacity of our labor force. The 1963 Economic Report of the President made the very conservative estimate that for the fourth quarter of 1962 full employment would have meant a $30 to $40 billion increase.[7] Thirty-five billion dollars was only a little over 6 percent of the actual quarterly level. Many would consider even a 10 percent figure for the increase conservative. Certainly if we were to raise our national output to a capacity level by increasing aggregate demand to a full capacity level, we would increase it substantially.

But an estimate of this sort would take account only of the direct gain in output. There is at least the possibility of an indirect increase in output, too. And some way might well be found to realize it. In large part because we have had inadequate levels of aggregate demand, various make-work devices have come into being that help to "make the work go around." The most obvious of these are efficiency hampering requirements imposed by, or at least instigated by trade unions, such measures as full-crew laws and other feather-bedding arrangements, also rules that require that a particular operation be performed by a member of a particular union. But there are make-work arrangements for which the professions are responsible, too. And to some extent at least sales effort by business enterprises can be considered a device for "making the work go around."

Inadequate aggregate demand is not the only reason why we have various make-work inefficiencies in the way our economy operates, but it is an important one. If we eliminate it, we should be able to find means of getting rid of some of the inefficiencies. It is not possible to say how much of a gain in output this would yield, in part because there would be some inefficiencies connected with a full-capacity level of output. But a far more important consideration is that the make-work inefficiencies might be very difficult to get rid of. However, certainly as things stand they substantially restrict the amount of our national output.

[7] See page X. The estimated increase is for the seasonally adjusted annual rate.

One of the gains from full employment would be a gain in avoided costs. It cannot well be compared objectively with the gains in added output, since the costs that would be avoided are psychological. However, some people would surely deem the cost-saving more important than the output gains. The costs that would be avoided are the costs of involuntary unemployment. Being unemployed because of a deficiency in aggregate demand means the painful and demoralizing activity of seeking work (if there is any hope of finding it) and being repeatedly told: "You are not wanted." Being involuntarily unemployed means spending whatever funds one has to begin with while they last, and when those funds are gone the disgrace of becoming a private or public burden. Prolonged involuntary unemployment is an experience that often causes serious mental illness. But I do not need to elaborate the costs of unemployment. Avoiding them would truly be a great gain.

The proposals I have made for achieving full employment constitute a radical program. Something quite different from the leisurely and easy-going policy we have been following is clearly needed if we are to reduce frictional unemployment to a minimum and eliminate both the business cycle and any remaining secular deficiency in aggregate demand. Quite frequently a radical economic change involves a good deal in the way of transitional costs. In particular there are likely to be large uncertainties in regard to the law that hamper business commitments until they have been resolved by judicial interpretations. And the immediate effect of a radical change may be unearned capital gains for some, unwarranted capital losses for others. Probably no radical economic change is possible without some transitional costs. But the program I have proposed is designed to minimize them. I think the transitional costs its inauguration would entail would be of no great consequence.

The program I have proposed would be an important step in the direction of making the economic system of the United States a managed economy. In considering any such step we must clearly be concerned about what it would mean for our personal freedoms and for our free enterprise type of economic organization.

The implications of the program for our personal freedoms relate primarily to the freedom of consumer's choice. The timing of major durable consumer goods purchases would be influenced by the Definite Period Agreements; the purchases of minor consumer durables by the busy period tax and the slack period tax credit. But these parts of the program would not exert any influence on the kinds of durables consumers would buy. And if there were a secular deficiency in aggregate demand and an income subsidy, consumers' free choice would determine the composition of most of the addition the subsidy would make to our G.N.P. On the whole, the role of consumers' free choices would be enhanced. Beyond this probably the principal significance for personal freedoms of the program I have proposed is that under it some people would have job opportunities and payroll incomes that they would not have otherwise.

In considering the implications of this program for our free enterprise economy let me recall the language used by Lord Keynes that I quoted in the first chapter. The program should leave it to "private self-interest . . . [to] determine what in particular is produced, in what proportions the factors of production will be combined to produce it, and how the value of the final product will be distributed between them." The program I have offered you does just this. The composition of the entire national product, including capital formation would, except for the changes in timing, continue to be determined much as it is today. Prices, market adjustments, and the profit system would continue to have much the same dominant parts in organizing activity they do now. The cycle would be ironed out and the economy would operate continuously at a capacity level. But essentially as wide a range of freedom of enterprise as we have at present would be maintained.

I hope when you have carefully considered my six proposals you will agree that full employment is a definite possibility under our free enterprise type of economic organization.

Index

Aggregate demand, 23, 29–30, 32–33, 35, 44, 67; *see also* Export surplus; Government G.N.P. expenditures; Inadequate aggregate demand; Personal consumption expenditures; Private capital formation
Annual wage, 10
Appalachia program, 15
Appropriations for shelf projects, 48
Attrition measures and structural unemployment, 13–15

Beveridge, William H., 3, 32, 64, 72
Bonuses, 35–36, 41–43, 46, 49, 63
Boondoggles, 65
Budget, economic, 32, 34
Budget of the Federal Government, 32, 71; *see also* Costs of proposed full-employment program
Buffer stock plan, 54–63
Built-in fiscal countercycle, 19
Bureau of Labor Statistics, 4, 12
Business cycles or business fluctuations, 21, 23, 28, 34, 44, 51–53, 63, 69, 70–71; *see also* Business recession possibilities; Inadequate aggregate demand
Business durable goods purchases, 21, 34, 44
Business recession or business contraction possibilities, 20–21

Capacity of the economy as limited by the size and quality of the labor force, 7, 9, 30
Capacity of the economy as limited by existing plant and equipment, 10, 29
Capacity level of operation, 9, 16, 22, 23, 27, 29–30, 33, 53, 69, 73, 77
Capacity utilization, 29, 68
Capital budget, 71
Capital formation quotas, 36
Ceiling prices, 55–56, 58–62
Collective bargaining agreements, 10, 14, 74
Commodity bales, 57–62
Commodity brokers, 60
Commodity stabilization proposal, 54–63
Construction, new private, 21, 34, 44
Consumer durable goods purchases, 21, 34, 44, 76
Consumption, *see* Personal consumption expenditures; Consumer durable goods purchases
Copeland, Morris A., 35–36, 40, 46, 64, 71
Cost-push inflation, 23, 32
Costs of proposed full-employment program, 54, 69–73, 75
Council of Economic Advisors, 2

Credit policy, *see* Federal Reserve credit policy
Creeping inflation, 23, 25

Deficit financing, 31–32
Definite period agreements, 35–37, 47, 76
Demand-pull inflation, 23, 33
Derived demand for capital goods, 64
Distressed areas, 15

Economic Report of the President, 1, 5, 6, 9, 12, 73
Education of the labor force, 5–7, 11
Employment Act of 1946, 2, 3, 19
Escalator clauses, 25
Excess capacity, 7, 28
Export surplus, 64
Featherbedding, 14–15, 74
Federal Government G.N.P. expenditures, 31, 34, 65
Federal Reserve credit policy, 20–21, 30–31, 37
Financial structure of the economy, 19
Fiscal policy, 31, 38, 39; *see also* Taxes; Tax credits; Subsidies; Income subsidy
Formula flexibility, 39
Freedom of consumers' choice, 66, 76
Freedom of enterprise, 3, 11, 13, 16–17, 22, 25, 29–30, 62, 76–77
Full employment, *see* Capacity level of operation

Gains from proposed full-employment program, 54, 73–75
General Services Administration, 50
G.N.P. Scheduling Agency, 35, 51, 57, 67, 69; *see also* Definite period agreements; Shelf project agreements; Stable inventory agreements
Government G.N.P. expenditures, 65; *see also* Federal Government G.N.P. expenditures

Graham, Benjamin, 18, 54–58, 61–62, 64
Gross National Product, *see* Aggregate demand

Hildebrand, George H., 15

Inadequate aggregate demand, 4, 28, 31–32, 34, 38, 44, 51, 52, 68
Income subsidy, 66–68, 76
Inflation, 22–25
In-service training, 11
International Bank for Reconstruction and Development, 56
International Monetary Fund, 56
International Commodity Stabilization Corporation, 56–62
International stabilization proposal, 54–63
Inventories and instability, *see* International stabilization proposal; Stable inventory agreements
Inventory increment, 34, 40, 44

Job Corps, 15
Joint Economic Committee, 4

Kaldor, Nicholas, 72
Keynes, John Maynard, 16–17, 19, 29, 33, 76

Labor force, reduction of size of, 17–18
Labor mobility, 8
Labor turnover, 11–12
Log-rolling, 65

Made-work, 15
Making the work go around, 74
Managed economy, 2, 76
Market adjustments, *see* Freedom of enterprise
Marshall, Alfred, 25
Merit rating basis for employer taxes, 10
Minimum wage, 11, 15
Military training, 50

Monetary policy, *see* Federal Reserve credit policy

Multiplier effect, 51

Mutual reinforcement aspect of proposed measures, 51, 54

Personal consumption expenditures, 64–67; *see also* Consumer durable goods purchases

Personal income, 52, 64–67, 76

Pierson, John H. G., 64–69

Policy, countercyclical, *see* Buffer stock plan; Definite period agreements; Fiscal policy; Income subsidy; Stable inventory agreements; Subsidies; Tax credits; Taxes; Works projects shelf

Pork-barrel, 65

Private capital formation, 44, 64–65, 68; *see also* Construction, new private; Consumer durable goods purchases; Inventory increment

Production for a market, 21

Profit system, *see* Freedom of enterprise

Promotional rates, 42

Psychological costs of unemployment, 75

Quarterly fiscal adjustments, 34

Salant, William A., 72

Sales effort by the G.N.P. Scheduling Agency, 37, 44, 49

Samuelson, Paul A., 23

Sapir, Michael, 2

Say's Law, 68

Secular deficiency in aggregate demand, 34, 52, 54, 63, 68–69, 72–73

Separation wage, 13

Shelf projects agreements, 46–50

Solow, Robert M., 23

Stable inventory agreements, 40–43, 47

State employment services, 11

Steering-wheel policy, 32–33

Stockpiling, *see* Buffer stock plan

Subsidies, 14, 31, 41–42; *see also* Income subsidy

Sufficient-stimulus full employment proposals, 32–33

Support prices, 55–56, 58–62

Tax credits, 35–36, 37–38, 69, 76

Taxes, 10, 14, 31, 36, 37–38, 66–67, 69, 76

Technological unemployment, *see* Unemployment, structural

Training of the labor force, 5, 7, 11

Unemployment, between-job, 3, 12

Unemployment, duration of, 9, 11

Unemployment, first-job-seeker, 3, 10–11

Unemployment, frictional, 3–6, 16, 53; *see also* Unemployment, between-job; Unemployment, first-job-seeker; Unemployment percentage; Unemployment, seasonal; Unemployment, structural; Unemployment, worker-type overpricing

Unemployment percentage, actual and unavoidable minimum, 1–4, 9, 26; *see also* Unemployment, frictional

Unemployment resulting from an inadequate level of aggregate demand, *see* Inadequate aggregate demand

Unemployment, seasonal, 3, 10

Unemployment, structural, 3, 8–9, 13–15

Unemployment, worker-type overpricing, 15–16

V-J Day Forecast, 2

Vocational guidance, 11–12

Working life, 17–18

Works projects shelf, 44–50, 67, 69

Work year, 17–18

W.P.A., 45, 50

Yntema, Theodore, 2–3